EXPLORE AUSTRALIA

TOP SPO[T]

FUN FACTS

PACKED WITH AWESOME STUFF!

THE KID EDITION

JANINE SCOTT

EXPLORE
AUSTRALIA

I can't wait to go exploring!

CONTENTS

Me too! This is way better than school!

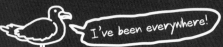
I've been everywhere!

PLACES I HAVE SEEN

AUSTRALIA

The great land of Terra Australis (aka Australia) is well worth exploring. In fact, it has had its fair share of enthusiastic but often eccentric explorers. Burke and Wills crossed Australia from south to north but died on the return journey. Charles Sturt set off to find a great salt lake in the centre of Australia, but found only a scorching desert. Matthew Flinders sailed in leaky ships on his quest to be the first to map Australia's coastline. He completed his mapping mission, but left the interior of Australia blank!

Timor Sea

PURNULULU

NINGALOO

WA

NULLARBOR

Indian Ocean

There are so many things to see and do!

PERTH

You'll have a whale of a time in Perth!

Southern Ocean

iv

WEIRD PLACE NAMES

Each country has its fair share of weird place names, and Australia is no exception — ever heard of Humpty Doo, Banana or Lake Massacre? But no matter how ridiculous or gruesome some names may seem, there's often a very sensible explanation. For example, the names Useless Inlet, Cape Tribulation, Disappointment Hill and Hopeless Reach were the result of discouraged and annoyed explorers. Read on to discover the stories behind some of the other weird place names on this vast continent.

RUM JUNGLE, NT
This place got its name for two reasons: there was a bit of jungle in the area and the local hotel served only rum!

HUMPTY DOO, NT
No, this town isn't related to Humpty Dumpty. Some people think it's named after the expression 'everything is humpty doo', which means 'everything is going well'.

MONKEY MIA, WA
This place, on the central western coast of Australia, is famous for dolphins — not monkeys! One possible explanation for the cute name is that Malay pearlers who worked in the area may have had pet monkeys.

* MONKEY MIA

WA

SUCCESS, WA
This suburb in southern Perth is a big hit! It is named after the HMS *Success*, a vessel from the early 1800s.

COWARD SPRINGS, SA
Are these springs named after a coward? No ... well, kind of. They were found in 1858 and named after Corporal Thomas Coward, who was a member of the party that discovered them.

* SUCCESS

ANXIOUS BAY, SA
Navigator Matthew Flinders was feeling anxious when he named this place in 1802. Mind you, he had good reason: his ship got trapped for a night on the shoreline.

COFFIN BAY, SA
You might think that many people died in this bay, but no: Vice-Admiral Sir Isaac Coffin just had an unfortunate name. Matthew Flinders named the bay in Coffin's honour in 1802.

POINT DANGER, NSW, NT, QLD, SA, VIC
It's no surprise that Australia has more than one Point Danger. After all, it can be a dangerous place.

I don't even live there!

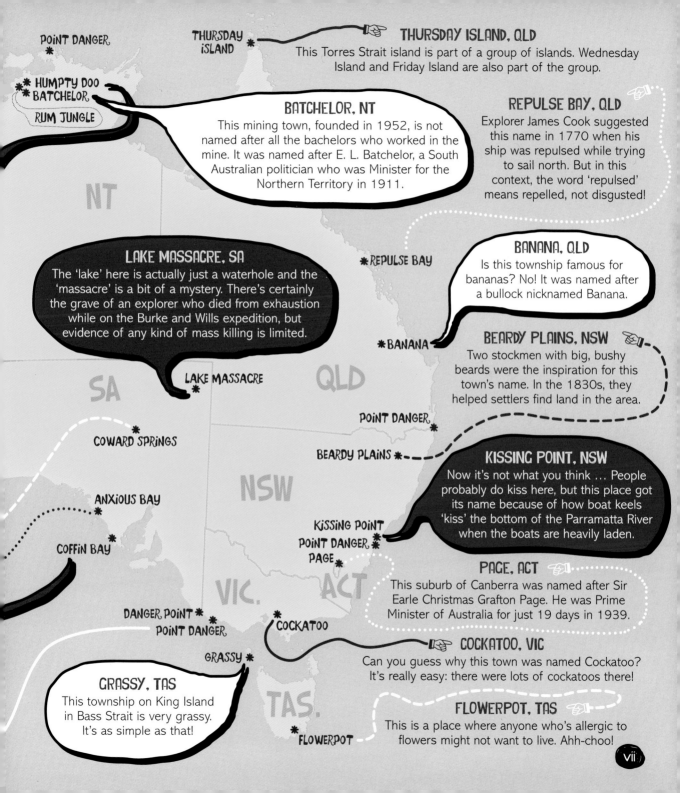

ABORIGINAL PLACE NAMES

Torres Strait Islanders and Aboriginal peoples were the first inhabitants of Australia. Today there are more than 500 different clans and many different languages. Places all over Australia have Aboriginal names, many of which describe the natural features of an area. However, some of the names' meanings remain uncertain. For instance, Berrimah, a suburb of Darwin, is a Mullukmulluk Aboriginal word that possibly means 'place where sick man gets better'!

Kurrohmin?

AROONA CREEK, NT
The word 'aroona' comes from the Aboriginal word 'alcaroona', which means 'running water'.

WA

ORROROO, SA
This town's name has an unusual meaning. It comes from the Ngadjuri Aboriginal term 'ar-ru', which translates to 'come on'!

GIDGEGANNUP, WA
This place name comes from the Nyungar Aboriginal term that means 'where spears are obtained'. Quick, duck!

GIDGEGANNUP
*

TAMBELLUP
*

TAMBELLUP, WA
This township's name possibly comes from the Nyungar Aboriginal word 'toombelarup', meaning 'thunder'.

KAPUNDA, SA
You might not feel the best in Kapunda. Some people believe its name comes from the Kaunda Aboriginal word 'kappi', which means 'vomit'!

WAGGA WAGGA, NSW
The Wiradhuri Aboriginal word 'wagga' means 'many crows'. No prizes for guessing what animal was common when this place was named!

Is that thunder or Kapunda?

MERBEIN, VIC
If you like throwing things, then this is the place for you. Merbein comes from a Keramin Aboriginal term that means 'throwing a stick'.

Babinda's name comes from the Yidiny Aboriginal word 'binda', meaning 'waterfall', probably because there are lots of waterfalls nearby. But it might also be because the town gets over 4 metres of rain annually.

BANYO, QLD
Banyo comes from a Gabi-Gabi Aboriginal word that means 'ridge'.

MOOROOKA, QLD
The Gabi-Gabi Aboriginal term 'mooroo', meaning 'nose', is the basis of this Brisbane suburb's name. No-one's really sure why, but it's possibly because the nearby Brisbane River cuts a bulbous shape into the landscape.

INDOOROOPILLY, QLD
Watch out in this Brisbane suburb … It got its name from the Gabi-Gabi Aboriginal word 'yinduru-pilli', which means 'gully of leeches'.

BOGGABILLA, NSW
This place name derives from the word 'bagaaaybila', a Kamilaroi Aboriginal word meaning 'full of creeks'.

CURRUMBIN, QLD
This place is named after the Banjalang Aboriginal word 'kurrohmin', which means 'kangaroo'.

COLLARENEBRI, NSW
Collarenebri is a Kamilaroi Aboriginal name that comes from the word 'galarriinbaraay', meaning 'eucalyptus blossoms'.

BOOLAROO, NSW
It might be a good idea to take some flyspray if you visit here. The word 'boolaroo' is an Awabakal Aboriginal term that means 'many flies'.

LEONGATHA, VIC
This town's name will make you smile: it comes from the Boonwurrung Aboriginal word 'liangatha', which means 'our teeth'.

BRIAGOLONG, VIC
This town gets its name from a Ganay Aboriginal word. It means 'men of the west'.

WOOLLOOMOOLOO, NSW
Some people believe this Dharuk Aboriginal word means 'kangaroos'.

AROONA CREEK

NT

QLD

BABINDA

SA

ORROROO

KAPUNDA

MERBEIN

NSW

INDOOROOPILLY

BOGGABILLA

COLLARENEBRI

WAGGA WAGGA

WOOLLOOMOOLOO

BANYO
MOOROOKA
CURRUMBIN

BOOLAROO

VIC.

ACT

LEONGATHA

BRIAGOLONG

TAS.

Quick, run!

DANGEROUS ANIMALS

Australia is the world's sixth largest country in area, which means there are plenty of wide, open spaces for animals to hop, jump, run, fly, slither and slide. Since many of the world's most dangerous animals call Australia home, luckily all that space also means there's plenty of room for people to run, escape and hide!

BOX JELLYFISH
FOUND: TROPICAL AUSTRALIAN COASTAL WATERS FROM WA THROUGH NT AND QLD

Box jellyfish are called sea wasps. The Australian box jellyfish has the deadliest sting of them all. What a champ!

WA

KANGAROO
FOUND: AUSTRALIA-WIDE

It might pay to hop out of a kangaroo's way. Kangaroos are very good kickboxers. Kapow!

DINGO
FOUND: CENTRAL AUSTRALIA, MOST OF NT, PARTS OF QLD, FRASER ISLAND

Dingoes are wild dogs that don't bark — they howl. But you won't hear them howling in Tasmania. Why? Because they never got established there.

RED-BACK SPIDER
FOUND: AUSTRALIA-WIDE

The male red-back spider has a white stripe on its back. The female red-back has a yellow-to-red stripe. Confusing, eh?

PERTH

PORTUGUESE MAN-OF-WAR (BLUE BOTTLE)
FOUND: EAST COAST BUT ALSO IN COASTAL WATERS OFF SA AND WA

Don't be fooled if you see a dead Portuguese man-of-war on the beach. It can still give you a sharp, painful sting!

SMOOTH STINGRAY
FOUND: SOUTHERN AUSTRALIAN WATERS

A group of stingrays is called a squadron, so a group of smooth stingrays might be called trouble! They are armed with a venomous spine.

VULNERABLE

INLAND TAIPAN SNAKE
FOUND: HADDON CORNER

The inland taipan snake is the deadliest land snake in the world, with enough venom in one drop to kill about 100 adult humans.

GREAT WHITE SHARK
FOUND: SOUTHERN AUSTRALIAN WATERS

The great white shark is also known as the 'white death'. These sharks have up to 300 teeth, but they do not chew their food. Manners, please!

DARWIN

SALTWATER CROC
FOUND: COASTAL AREAS OF NORTHERN AUSTRALIA

Saltwater crocodiles have a mighty bite. Indeed, it's the greatest bite pressure of any living animal. Crunch, munch, lunch!

CANE TOAD
FOUND: PREDOMINANTLY NORTHERN QUEENSLAND BUT MOVING ACROSS TO NT

Cane toads are poisonous, so listen out for them. The males can sound like old diesel boat motors!

REEF STONEFISH
FOUND: GREAT BARRIER REEF, QLD, FAR NORTHERN NSW

Is 13 an unlucky number? It is if you meet a reef stonefish. They have 13 fin spines that inject poisonous venom.

VULNERABLE

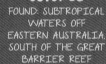

SOUTHERN CASSOWARY
FOUND: NORTHERN QLD

No wonder the female southern cassowary is flightless – its claim to fame is that it is Australia's heaviest bird!

BULL ANT
FOUND: AUSTRALIA-WIDE

Bull ants are aggressive and have painful venomous stings. Ants in your pants are not recommended!

BLUE-LINED OCTOPUS
FOUND: SUBTROPICAL WATERS OFF EASTERN AUSTRALIA, SOUTH OF THE GREAT BARRIER REEF

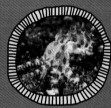

If you see blue lines on the body of a blue-lined octopus, it's having a bad day. Blue means 'back off, bucko'!

EASTERN BROWN SNAKE
FOUND: EAST COAST

Of all land snakes, the eastern brown snake has the second most toxic venom. When provoked, it can rear up and form the letter 'S'. S-s-s-scary!

NT

SA

SYDNEY FUNNEL-WEB SPIDER
FOUND: SYDNEY, PARTS OF NSW

The venom of the Sydney funnel-web spider can be deadly to humans, but harmless to cats, dogs and guinea pigs!

QLD

BRISBANE

NSW

ADELAIDE

CANBERRA

SYDNEY

VIC.

ACT

MELBOURNE

TIGER SHARK
FOUND: SOUTHERN AUSTRALIAN WATERS

Tiger sharks like to eat just about anything – including people and rubbish! No wonder they have the nickname 'wastebasket of the sea'.

TAS

HOBART

RED-BELLIED BLACK SNAKE
FOUND: NORTHERN QLD, EASTERN NSW AND VIC

Red-bellied black snakes are deadly to humans. Luckily, they are shy snakes that would rather slip away from danger.

FUN FACTS

AUSTRALIA IS REALLY BIG! HOW BIG? THIS BIG!

MELVILLE ISLAND
Australia has 8222 islands! Melville Island is the largest, covering 5786 square kilometres.

GANTHEAUME POINT
Here you'll find dinosaur footprints over 130 million years old.

STRELLEY POOL
See the world's oldest fossil. It's 3.4 billion years old.

WA

WOLFE CREEK CRATER
Second largest meteorite crater in the world.

MOUNT AUGUSTUS
Twice the size of Uluru, and the world's LARGEST monocline.

MEEBERRIE
The strongest onshore earthquake was recorded here on 29 April 1941. It measured a magnitude of 7.2.

OODNADATTA
Hottest recorded temperature in Australia, 50.7°C on 2 January 1960.

BUSSELTON
Walk along the longest timber-piled jetty in the Southern Hemisphere.

SOS!

OVER 8000 SHIPWRECKS!

KAKADU NATIONAL PARK

. . . has the world's largest concentration of rock art, with over 5000 recorded sites!

POPULATIONS

People 23.8 million

Cattle 29.3 million

Sheep 75.5 million

Camels 300,000

Kangaroos 50 million

WORLD'S LARGEST LIVING STRUCTURE AT 2,300 KILOMETRES LONG

GREAT BARRIER REEF

NT

QLD

PALM VALLEY
FINKE GORGE NATIONAL PARK

Home to roughly 12,000 red cabbage palms found nowhere else on the planet!

HADDON CORNER

The inland taipan snake lives here and is the most poisonous snake in the world, but there are no recorded fatalities.

HOTTEST!

SA

WETTEST!

KATI THANDA-LAKE EYRE

Largest salt lake in Australia and, at 15.2 metres below sea level, the lowest point in Australia.

CROHAMHURST

Most rainfall (907 milimetres) recorded in a day in Australia, 3 February 1893.

ORANGE

One of the first places gold was discovered, 1851.

Wet and wild!

ANNA CREEK STATION

This is the largest working cattle station in the world, 23,677 square kilometres.

Highest point in Australia: 2228 metres

MOUNT KOSCIUSZKO

NSW

ACT

HYAMS BEACH

Whitest sand on Earth.

COLDEST!

BENDIGO

Home to the longest (Sun Loong) and oldest (Loong) imperial dragons in the world!

VIC.

CHARLOTTE PASS

Coldest recorded temperature in Australia, −23°C on 29 June 1994.

BALLARAT

The world's largest alluvial gold nugget was found here. It was called 'The Welcome Stranger' and weighs 70 kilograms!

NABOWLA

Home to Bridestowe, the world's largest commercial lavender farm.

THE AUSTRALIAN COASTLINE
IS 24,218 KILOMETRES LONG!

TAS

NIGGLY CAVE

Deepest cave in Australia at 375m deep.

EXIT CAVE
SOUTH-WEST NATIONAL PARK

Don't get lost in the longest known cave in Australia at 23 kilometres long.

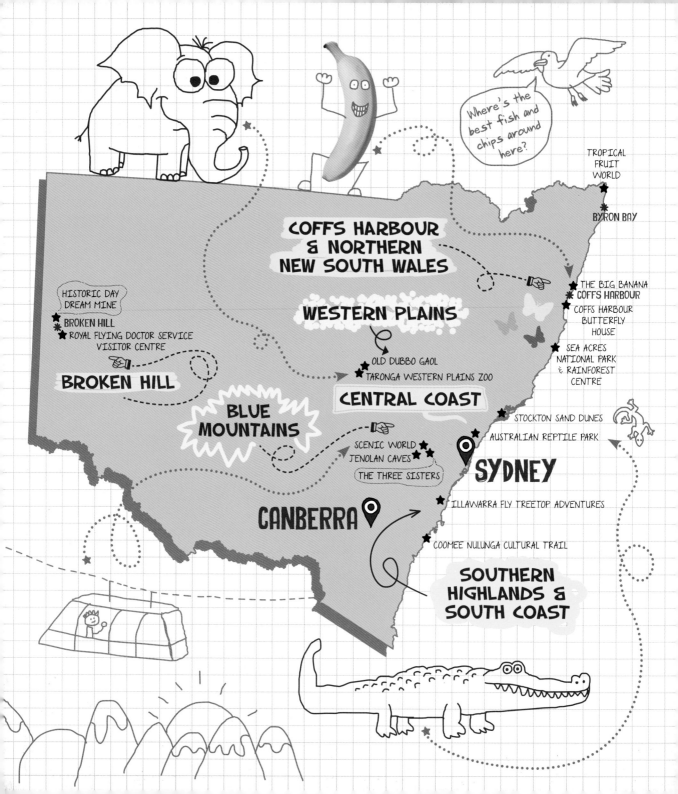

Where's the best fish and chips around here?

TROPICAL FRUIT WORLD

BYRON BAY

COFFS HARBOUR & NORTHERN NEW SOUTH WALES

THE BIG BANANA
COFFS HARBOUR

COFFS HARBOUR BUTTERFLY HOUSE

WESTERN PLAINS

SEA ACRES NATIONAL PARK & RAINFOREST CENTRE

HISTORIC DAY DREAM MINE
BROKEN HILL
ROYAL FLYING DOCTOR SERVICE VISITOR CENTRE

OLD DUBBO GAOL
TARONGA WESTERN PLAINS ZOO

BROKEN HILL

CENTRAL COAST

STOCKTON SAND DUNES

BLUE MOUNTAINS

AUSTRALIAN REPTILE PARK

SCENIC WORLD
JENOLAN CAVES
THE THREE SISTERS

SYDNEY

ILLAWARRA FLY TREETOP ADVENTURES

CANBERRA

COOMEE NULUNGA CULTURAL TRAIL

SOUTHERN HIGHLANDS & SOUTH COAST

So ... uh ... not the huge animals in the sea, right?

NEW SOUTH WHALES

largest city

Sydney is Australia's largest capital city in terms of population. But watch out Sydneysiders, because Melbourne is predicted to overtake Sydney. No need to panic just yet though: it may not happen until about 2053!

SYDNEY is Australia's oldest city. In 1788, when Captain Arthur Phillip and his fleet of 11 ships sailed into Port Jackson and then onto Sydney Cove, he didn't intend for it to be a great city. Its much less attractive purpose was to serve as a dumping ground for Britain's convicts! Despite this shaky start, however, Sydney became not just a great city, but a place renowned the world over.

Deepest harbour

Sydney Harbour's official name is Port Jackson. It is one of the deepest natural harbours in the world. Its deepest point is about 45 metres.

largest arch

The Sydney Harbour Bridge holds the record for the largest steel arch bridge in the world. The top of the arch is 134 metres above sea level – and kids ten and over can climb to the top (see p.7).

FUN FACTS

Strangest place name

Imagine coming to a place quite by chance while making your way to somewhere else. That's probably what happened at Come By Chance, a tiny town in northern NSW. So naming this place would have been a no-brainer!

Highest mountain

Mount Kosciuszko, in the Snowy Mountains, is Australia's highest mountain. It is 2228 metres above sea level, but don't let that stop you from getting to the top. You can catch a chairlift most of the way, then it's an easy 6-kilometre walk to the peak!

Quirkiest festival

The award for the quirkiest festival goes to the Stroud Brick and Rolling Pin Throwing Competition. Better watch where you stand at this event!

Smallest island

Snapper Island is the smallest island in Sydney Harbour. In the 1930s, the island had an extreme makeover: it was blasted and flattened into the shape of a naval ship! Presumably this had something to do with its connections to the Royal Australian Navy.

Oldest house

Elizabeth Farm in Rosehill is the oldest surviving European house in Sydney *and* Australia. It was built in 1793 for British army officer John Macarthur and was named after his wife Elizabeth.

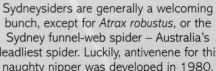

Deadliest spider

Sydneysiders are generally a welcoming bunch, except for *Atrax robustus*, or the Sydney funnel-web spider – Australia's deadliest spider. Luckily, antivenene for this naughty nipper was developed in 1980.

3

TOP SPOTS

SYDNEY

Australian National Maritime Museum

Australia is an ocean-loving nation. Its relationship with the sea goes back hundreds of years, although it has not always been plain sailing (if you'll pardon the pun). In 1770, for instance, the great explorer Captain James Cook had a near-fatal collision with the Great Barrier Reef, while in 1787, some of the British convicts on the First Fleet attempted a mutiny on the eight-month journey to Australia. More recently, during the Sydney Hobart Yacht Race in 1998, six sailors tragically died, five yachts sank and 55 sailors had to be rescued. The Australian National Maritime Museum brings these and other maritime tribulations (and triumphs) to life.

CRAZY BEACH BANS

It's hard to believe, but before 1902, it was illegal to swim at Sydney beaches in daylight hours! And it seems ridiculous now, but in the 1950s, some beaches had not only lifesavers, but swimsuit inspectors too. It was the inspectors' job to measure swimsuits and make sure they met strict regulations; bikinis were actually against the law! You can see what swimsuits used to look like at the museum, which also has a cool collection of surfboards and other beach toys.

VESSELS GALORE

The museum has one of the world's largest floating historical vessel collections, including a navy destroyer, a submarine and a replica of Captain Cook's HMB *Endeavour*. Some of the museum's vessels are on dry land, including a boat made out of beer cans! You can also explore the *Spirit of Australia* – the world's fastest boat.

WHAT'S IN A NAME?
Swimming costumes are called 'bathers' in Vic, SA, WA and Tas, 'cossie' or 'swimmers' in NSW and 'togs' in Qld. Go figure!

Bondi Beach

Bondi Beach wasn't always a place where you could enjoy a leisurely swim. In the early 1800s, convicts were forbidden to swim there (or in Sydney Harbour), partly due to the dangers of sharks and stingrays. Later, even settlers weren't allowed to swim at the beach; it was considered indecent to swim during the day, and for men and women to swim together! Luckily, the laws eventually relaxed and thousands flocked to Bondi Beach, which earned the nickname the 'Playground of the Pacific'.

RECORD RESCUE

The Bondi Surf Bathers' Life Saving Club was set up in February 1907 and its members have saved countless lives over the years. One of the club's biggest moments occurred on Sunday 6 February 1938, which became known as Black Sunday. That's because more than 300 people were rescued that day, after a series of huge waves swept them out to sea. Sadly though, five swimmers perished.

Cockatoo Island

Polly want a cracker? Uh. No thanks. I want my own island!

Cockatoo Island is the largest island in Sydney Harbour. Early inhabitants were sulphur-crested cockatoos. Then, from 1839 to 1869, its more famous residents were convicts, sent there to work for the colony by quarrying stone. They also built barracks and other prison buildings on the island. After the last convicts left, Cockatoo Island was not left dormant for long. In 1871 it became home to orphaned and delinquent girls. The girls might be considered the lucky ones though because 500 orphaned and wayward boys were forced to live on a ship moored off the island!

CONVICT CHALLENGE

As you explore the island, take the 'Convict Clues Challenge' and see if you can answer the secret convict questions. The activity booklet comes with a pull-out map, so it might be fun to bring a compass!

NASTY PAST-Y
For punishment, convicts were often tied to the island's rocky outcrops for days on end or made to climb into special underground punishment cells.

Well, this sucks!

Hyde Park Barracks Museum

Francis Greenway was a convict and the architect of the Hyde Park Barracks. Luckily for him, he received a pardon for his good work, but the 50,000 convict men and boys who lived in the barracks between 1813 and 1848 didn't get off so lightly. All they got was a hard home life and rats for roomies! Later, at various times, the barracks turned into a hostel for orphan girls, a depot for female immigrants and an asylum for aged and destitute women.

Hey! That's my bread!

RASCALLY RODENTS

This bread is delicious! It'll feed all 438 of my kids!

Rats and mice helped to preserve many of the residents' possessions, which are displayed at the museum. The rodents dragged items, such as clothes, buttons and toothbrushes, under the floorboards to use in their nests. Between 1979 and 1981, archaeologists found more than 100,000 items under the floor!

BEDS IN THE BARRACKS

Imagine sharing your bedroom with 600 others. The barracks housed about 600 convicts, but sometimes many, many more were squeezed in. The lucky ones got a hammock; the unlucky ones slept on the floor. Today, there are 106 replica hammocks that you can try out, along with leg irons and convict shirts. If you're feeling very brave, the museum holds sleepovers!

Oh rats! All I got today was a hanky and a toothbrush.

ROOM TO ROAM
Hyde Park is one of Australia's oldest public parks. You won't be short of a tree to climb here because there are more than 500 in the park.

RAT RACE

You can follow the 'Rats' Trail' through the museum to search for historical clues. You can also see carcasses of real rodent robbers (aka rats) on display – *ewwww!*

Sydney Harbour Bridge

An adventurous nine-year-old boy named Lennie Gwyther went the extra mile to attend the Sydney Harbour Bridge's opening in 1932. In fact, he went 600 extra miles. He rode alone on his pony, Ginger Mick, from Victoria to Sydney. On 19 March, about 750,000 people came to watch the opening and pageant. Lennie and his pony were such a hit in the news that they were invited to join the opening ceremony. The events of the day were truly dazzling, and that's probably why about 1000 people fainted!

Are we there yet, Dad?

SPANNER IN THE WORKS

As you stand safely on the bridge, spare a thought for the 16 workers who lost their lives during the bridge's construction. One poor guy fell backwards from the arch when his spanner slipped off a nut!

ACTION & ADVENTURE

If you are aged over ten and taller than 1.2 metres, you can climb to the top of the arch on a guided tour. Oh, and it helps to not be afraid of heights ...

1.2m
1m

SHOP TILL YOU DROP

The shopping list for the Harbour Bridge would have included:

* six million rivets
* 95,000 cubic metres of concrete
* 52,800 tonnes of steel
* 40,000 blocks of granite
* 272,000 litres of paint

ONE SHADE OF GREY

Take note of the bridge's grey paint. The paint was mixed specially for the bridge and has the official name, 'Bridge Grey'. When it was built, some Sydney residents thought the bridge should be called the Rainbow Bridge and be painted with rainbow colours!

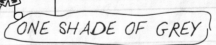

Sydney Opera House

Bennelong Point, the site where the famous Sydney Opera House sits, was once the home of a humble tram depot and old tram sheds. In 1956 there was a competition to design an opera house at this site for the city of Sydney. The winning architect, Jørn Utzon, was one of 233 contestants. At first, his design landed in the reject pile, but luckily for Australia, renowned American architect Eero Saarinen rescued it, saying it was genius. The United Nations thought so too: in 2007 the Sydney Opera House was listed as a World Heritage site.

LUNCHTIME LYRICS

Today, about 3000 events are held at the Opera House each year. In 1960, Paul Robeson (an American performer) put on the first unofficial concert. His 'stage' was the scaffolding and his audience was the construction workers who ate their lunches as he sang.

OPERA ANCESTOR

In 1879 there was another Sydney Opera House. It opened in a warehouse on the corner of King and York streets. By 1900 it was a little worse for wear and was condemned.

BEHIND THE SCENES

Have you ever wanted to go backstage and peek into a star's dressing room? You can on the Opera House's Junior Tour.

WEIRD WILDLIFE

Not all performances at the Opera House went to plan. In the 1980s, during the opera *Boris Godunov*, a live chicken that was part of the show strutted off the stage and landed on top of a cello player!

Ready or not, here I come!

Taronga Zoo

Climbing is so much fun!

The first public zoo in Sydney (and NSW) was built in 1884 on land fittingly known as Billy Goat Swamp. The zoo soon outgrew this site and in 1912 it was granted new land. The elephants and many other animals travelled on a barge across Sydney Harbour — a scene that would no doubt have rivalled Noah's Ark! — to their new home at Taronga Zoo. In total, 552 birds, 228 mammals and 64 reptiles became the new zoo's first residents.

ACTION & ADVENTURE

Wild Ropes in the surrounds of Taronga Zoo is a high-ropes adventure course that has bridges, tunnels, aerial rock-climbing walls and flying foxes. It's the closest thing to feeling like a monkey!

What a view!

TIDY ANIMALS

The keepers at Taronga Zoo keep the enclosures clean for the animals. Imagine the keepers' astonishment when Lulu, an ex-circus chimp, grabbed a broom and started sweeping her own enclosure when she first arrived at the zoo in 1965!

GREAT APE ESCAPE

All the animals are safe in their enclosures at Taronga Zoo these days, but there have been some daring escapes in the past. Like in the mid-1950s, when Koko the chimpanzee escaped and jumped inside an unlocked car parked at the zoo. To capture her, the keepers poured chloroform, which works like an anaesthetic, in through a small window gap. Zzz!

EXPLORE MORE

SYDNEY

GRRRR!!!

Australian Museum

The Australian Museum has been curating objects for more than 175 years – which may explain why it has more than 18 million objects in its collection. One of its prized possessions is a Tasmanian tiger pup preserved in a bottle. Some of the individual collections are so large it's been suggested that they may need a clean out or a garage sale – although we're not sure how many people would line up to buy something from the 635,000-specimen spider collection!

Dinosaur displays

The museum has ten complete dinosaur skeletons and eight life-size models. Winny the dinosaur puppet lives at the museum and is based on a three-year-old muttaburrasaurus, which was a plant-eating Australian dinosaur. The muttaburrasaurus is named after the Queensland town of Muttaburra where its fossil remains were first found in the 1960s.

Frozen in time

One collection at the museum is frozen – although not exactly like the ice cubes in your freezer … The frozen-tissue collection contains DNA and tissue samples of different species from around the world, including whales from southern Australian waters and bats from Papua New Guinea.

NASTY PAST-Y

William Holmes, the first custodian of the museum, had an unfortunate accident in 1831. Just two years after getting the job, he accidentally shot and killed himself while collecting birds in Queensland!

He shot to fame!

Luna Park

Luna Park's enormous smiling face welcomes visitors to Sydney's beloved theme park. On opening night, 4 October 1935, neon lights flashed on and off in the eyes, the eyebrows moved up and down and laughter was broadcast from the base of the entrance towers. The famous face has had a number of makeovers since then, including one that gave it a lumpy forehead and bloodshot eyeballs! In 1953, artist Arthur Barton redesigned and reconstructed it, modelling its happy expression on Old King Cole, the merry old soul. The face you see today was created in 1995 and is based on Barton's creation.

Teeth terror

In July 1974, robbers changed the appearance of Luna Park's entrance. They stole six of the teeth from the face's open mouth!

Adrenaline rush

There are loads of cool rides at Luna Park. With names like Devil's Drop, Hair Raiser, Whirly Wheel and Wonky Walk, you are sure to have plenty of heart-hopping moments!

I'm no dummy!

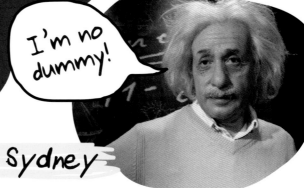

Madame Tussauds Sydney

This is where famous Australian musicians, sports and movie stars, leaders and an outlaw rub shoulders with some of the world's most popular people. Even though the wax models don't move, it doesn't mean you can't. You can wear Ned Kelly's suit of armour and join his gang, sit in a replica of Mark Webber's Formula 1 car and sing your heart out on stage with pop princess Kylie Minogue!

Hands-on

Experience wax making first-hand at Madame Tussauds – quite literally. You can get your own hand immortalised in wax!

SELFIE SPOT

You are allowed to touch the wax figures, so grab your camera, throw your arm around your favourite star and say 'smile!' ... oops, one of you can't smile!

Powerhouse Museum

At the Powerhouse, curiosity and creativity go hand in hand. Science and art are the broad topics of this museum, with collections that feature costumes, transport, furniture, technology, music and space. The museum's name came about because it moved in 1988 to the Ultimo Powerhouse, which was Sydney's first public power station, supplying power to the city's new electric trams in the early 1900s.

Priceless possession

The Powerhouse has about 500,000 items, but many of them are not on display, such as the museum's most valuable item, the Boulton and Watt engine. This is the world's oldest rotative (wheel-turning) steam engine and it is priceless. In 1887 in London, the machine was headed for the scrapyards. Luckily, Professor Liversidge of Sydney University rescued it.

Q Station

Q Station is short for Quarantine Station. From 1833, migrant ship passengers who were thought to have a contagious disease had to be quarantined for about 40 days when they arrived in Australia, to prevent the spread of disease. In the early days, people slept in tents. Today the site, on North Head, is supposed to be haunted by some of the 500 people who died of diseases such as Spanish influenza, smallpox, typhus and bubonic plague.

Isolate & separate

In all, about 580 ships were detained at North Head and more than 13,000 people were put in isolation. Plants and animals were not immune; they could also be quarantined!

NASTY PAST-Y
Between 1837 and 1853, the first thing people saw when they arrived at the station were the burial grounds!

RIP

Sea Life Sydney Aquarium

With exhibit names like Dugong Island, Shark Walk, South Coast Shipwreck and Bay of Rays, you know you're in for a watery adventure at Sea Life Sydney Aquarium. Get up close and personal with resident dugongs Pig and Wuru at Dugong Island (did you know dugongs are related to elephants?). Walk over the top of more than 40 sharks on Shark Walk's glass walkway (don't worry — they can't bite through the glass!). You can even snorkel in a safe, see-through enclosure and come face to face with reef sharks and other fish.

Danger zone

There are different zones in the aquarium. Some of the animals in the zones are dangerous, such as the sharks, stingrays and platypuses (which can kill a small dog!). In the hands-on discovery rock pool, the animals aren't exactly cute and cuddly, but they are at least harmless.

I'm Natalie ... err Napoleon!

I'm 'armless!

WEIRD WILDLIFE
One boy fish at the aquarium used to be a girl fish. Napoleon is a Napoleon wrasse. This species can change from a female to a male, but not vice versa. Before the change, the fish's name was Natalie!

A jaw dropper

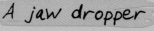

Not all sharks are aggressive. Take a look at the giant grey nurse sharks in the aquarium. These sharks are a placid species, earning them the nickname 'labradors of the sea'.

Sydney Observatory

There's more to this historical site than just stargazing in the southern skies. In its long, important history, it has been used to keep time and weather records as well as to send signals to ships and the residents of Sydney. The Sydney Observatory sits on what is now called Observatory Hill, the highest point overlooking Sydney Harbour. However, when a flagstaff (flagpole) was built there in 1788, it was named Flagstaff Hill, and when a convict built a windmill on the site in 1796, it became known as Windmill Hill!

Star attraction

The planetarium at the Sydney Observatory is out of this world. Starry-eyed visitors can watch a sped-up night sky from dusk to dawn, search for constellations and observe Mars, the moon and distant galaxies.

Sydney Olympic Park

This is probably not going to appeal to couch potatoes! This entertainment and recreation venue was previously the site of a brickworks, an abattoir and chemical factories. Sadly, over time, the site turned into a polluted wasteland — that is until the 2000 Olympics came along. Thanks to newly established wetlands, parklands, planned urban areas and 8 million plants, the site has blossomed and was even made a suburb in its own right in 2009.

A 'to do' list

The list of things to do here is lo-o-o-o-ong! There's a skatepark, an aquatic centre, bike safari circuits, train rides and much, much more. Don't worry if you didn't pack a bike, a skateboard, a scooter or skates. You can hire them.

ACTION & ADVENTURE
Blaxland Riverside Park is the largest playground in Sydney. Found at Sydney Olympic Park, it also has the largest outdoor waterplay facility in NSW.

Sydney Tower

If you want a spectacular view of Sydney, then this is the place to be. Sydney Tower is twice the height of the Sydney Harbour Bridge. Step outside onto the Skywalk and feel the fear. On very windy days, the tower sways about 1 metre each way. Don't panic too much though: it is still considered one of the world's safest buildings.

Clean machine

Imagine washing Sydney Tower's windows. Luckily, a machine named Charlie cleans them. It takes Charlie two days to make the tower's 420 windows sparkle.

Twice the height of Sydney Harbour Bridge?! Whoa!

Wild winds

The Skywalk closes if winds are 80 kilometres per hour or stronger. That's comforting to know!

SELFIE SPOT
This is the perfect selfie spot, especially because the Sydney Tower is the first location in Sydney to see the sun rise and the last to see dusk.

EXPLORE MORE
BLUE MOUNTAINS

DON'T TOUCH

JENOLAN CAVES

An escaped convict and cattle rustler is believed to have been the first European to set foot in the Jenolan Caves, a limestone underworld that's one of the oldest cave systems on Earth. In the late 1830s, Irish outlaw James McKeown used the caves as a hide-out. Settlers described McKeown as a ruffian with a spear wound under his left eye! The cavern where the outlaw was captured became known as McKeown's Hole. The local Indigenous people, however, had known about the caves thousands of years earlier. At that time, they named them Binoomea, which means 'dark places'. The Aboriginal name Jenolan, meaning 'high mountain', was adopted in 1884.

LOOK, DON'T TOUCH

One of the rules for visitors to the caves is 'do not touch any rock or crystal'. Long ago, there was no such rule. Cave visitors used to snap off the limestone formations and take them home as souvenirs. Luckily, rock robbing was outlawed in 1872 – otherwise there might not be much left to look at today!

WHAT'S IN A NAME?
The blue haze from the oil that rises from the eucalyptus trees in the Blue Mountains gave the area its name.

CAVE CLEAN

The Orient Cave is a record breaker. It was the first cave in the world to get a steam clean!

COOL CAVES

Phew, I made it!

The temperature inside the caves is fairly constant throughout the year. It is about 15°C. However, your temperature might go up because all the caves have hundreds of steps. The River Cave has a whopping 1298 steps!

BREATHE IN

A tour for adventurous tweens, teens and adults is called the 'Plughole'. On it, you have to crawl and squeeze through parts of the cave. Amazingly, you do not need to be fit or thin – although it might help to breathe in!

SCENIC WORLD

The Scenic Railway, one of several attractions at Scenic World, has come a long way since 1878 when it used to transport miners and coal from the mines at Katoomba. By the early 1900s, bushwalkers in the area started to hitch (maybe even beg!) rides in the coal skip, and by 1928, a specially built train called the 'Mountain Devil' took weekend visitors for joy rides. Today, the world's steepest passenger railway has a 64-degree incline that will get your heart racing. No wonder the ride is called the 'Cliffhanger'.

IT'S THE B-EST

Lots of 'est' words describe the Scenic Cableway at Scenic World. It is the big*gest* cable car in Australia and also the steep*est* and larg*est* aerial cable car in the Southern Hemisphere.

THE THREE SISTERS

Imagine if your sister was turned to stone! Aboriginal legend has it that these three sandstone pillars were once beautiful sisters who were turned to stone by their father to keep them safe from a scary bunyip. The sisters were named Meehni, Wimlah and Gunnedoo. From Echo Point, you can take off down the Giant Stairway's 800-plus steps – carved from the mountainside in the early 1900s – to the base of the Three Sisters.

THREE CHEERS FOR STAIRS

The Giant Stairway was officially opened on 1 October 1932. As part of the ceremony, three men clambered up the rocks and planted an Australian flag on the second sister.

SELFIE SPOT
Pose on the Echo Point lookout and snap a 'family' photo of you and the Three Sisters.

Does it echo, echo, echo ... ?

EXPLORE MORE
BROKEN HILL

HISTORIC DAY DREAM MINE

Silverton, a town near Broken Hill, offers a clue as to what was mined here. You guessed it — silver! It was dangerous work for the miners, which included boys only about 14 or 15 years old (sometimes much younger). The boys had to hand pick the ore after it had been fired and sort it into boxes. Today, you can take a tour of the disused mine decked out with a miner's helmet and lamp. Make sure you keep your eyes peeled: there is still unmined silver about …

WHAT'S IN A NAME?

Broken Hill was named after a number of hills that looked as if they had a massive crack in them. However, the crack has long since been mined away!

ROYAL FLYING DOCTOR SERVICE VISITOR CENTRE

The Flying Doctor aerial ambulance service has changed a great deal since its first flight on 17 May 1928 when it had to hire a plane and pay two shillings for every mile it travelled. The service's first pilot flew in an open cockpit — chilly! He often landed in paddocks — bumpy! He was guided by landmarks, such as rivers, telegraph lines and fences — scary! At the visitor centre, you can see a working base in action, visit a hangar with aircraft inside it and learn loads about aero-medical history in the outback.

MEDICAL MEASUREMENTS

Each year, the pilots of the Royal Flying Doctor Service fly the equivalent of 25 round trips to the moon!

EXPLORE MORE
WESTERN PLAINS

OLD DUBBO GAOL

Imagine escaping from jail and being pursued down the main street by a warden sporting his dressing gown and slippers! There were many attempted and actual escapes from this prison. It possibly had something to do with the harsh surroundings and the tough treatment of prisoners by the jailers. On a guided tour, you can experience the law and lawlessness of the 1800s — be prepared for a prison warden to scold you and a prisoner to attempt to pick your pockets!

FUN FACTOR
Detectives and prisons go hand in hand. Become a super sleuth by answering questions about the jail as you walk around the grounds. Can you crack the code?

XXXVII

OLD DUBBO GAOL.

TARONGA WESTERN PLAINS ZOO

Wheels rather than feet are the way to explore this zoo. You can travel around the 6-kilometre one-way zoo circuit by car, electric cart or bicycle. This is definitely a zoo with a difference. You can even go on a 'zoofari', which is camping (or should that be glamping?) in a safari-style lodge inside the zoo.

NO BARRIERS
The animals aren't fenced in at the Western Plains Zoo, but don't worry: concealed moats keep the animals and visitors safely apart.

I love this free-range set-up!

EXPLORE MORE
COFFS HARBOUR & NORTHERN NEW SOUTH WALES

COFFS HARBOUR BUTTERFLY HOUSE

If you like wearing bright-coloured clothes and dabbing on sweet-smelling perfume, then watch out. The resident butterflies here often mistake people for flowers and use them as landing and launching pads! You can see many native butterflies here, including Australia's largest butterfly, the Cairns birdwing, which gets its name because its flight pattern looks like a bird.

WONDER OF WINGS

A newly hatched butterfly emerges from its chrysalis with damp wings that are like soggy, crumpled paper. After about an hour, its wings are dry and ready for flying.

Ouch! That's gotta hurt!

SEA ACRES NATIONAL PARK & RAINFOREST CENTRE

Is it a beach or a rainforest? Well, it's a place where the forest meets the sea at Port Macquarie. Wander along the elevated boardwalk that goes from the understorey layer of the tropical rainforest up to the canopy layer. From up there, you'll literally get a bird's-eye view of the many birds that dwell in the forest, such as brush turkeys, green catbirds and yellow robins.

TEETH GRIEF

Keep your eyes peeled at Sea Acres for the diamond python. This snake is not poisonous, but it can have a memorable bite: sometimes its teeth snap off and get stuck in its victim!

THE BIG BANANA

It's big, it's a banana and it's modelled on a big pineapple in Hawaii. The famous Big Banana at Coffs Harbour has a wooden frame and concrete-reinforced skin. It opened in 1964 and was created to attract customers to a roadside fruit stall that sold bananas grown on a nearby plantation. When thieves broke into the souvenir shop in 1967, among the things they stole were chocolate-coated frozen bananas!

MORE THAN BANANAS

Visitors will go bananas! As well as the water park, there's an ice-skating rink, laser-tag arena and minigolf course. Oh, and just about every banana-themed thing you can think of.

FUN FACTOR

Australia's first three-storey inflatable water slide is at the Big Banana's water park, appropriately named the Banana Slip Water Park!

TROPICAL FRUIT WORLD

You can eat a rainbow here. There are red, orange, yellow, green, blue, indigo and violet fruits, as well as many other weird and wonderful varieties. Ice-cream bean comes from Central and South America and its spongy white pulp tastes like vanilla ice-cream. Caramel fruit is from Brazil and has a creamy flesh that is the flavour of caramel. So get stuck in to all the tangy, tasty tucker at this delicious spot at Duranbah in far northern NSW.

SNACK SPOT

There are more than 500 varieties of fruit grown on the farm — that's a lot of fruit salad! The Bush Tucker garden features some native Australian plants, such as macadamias and Davidson's plums.

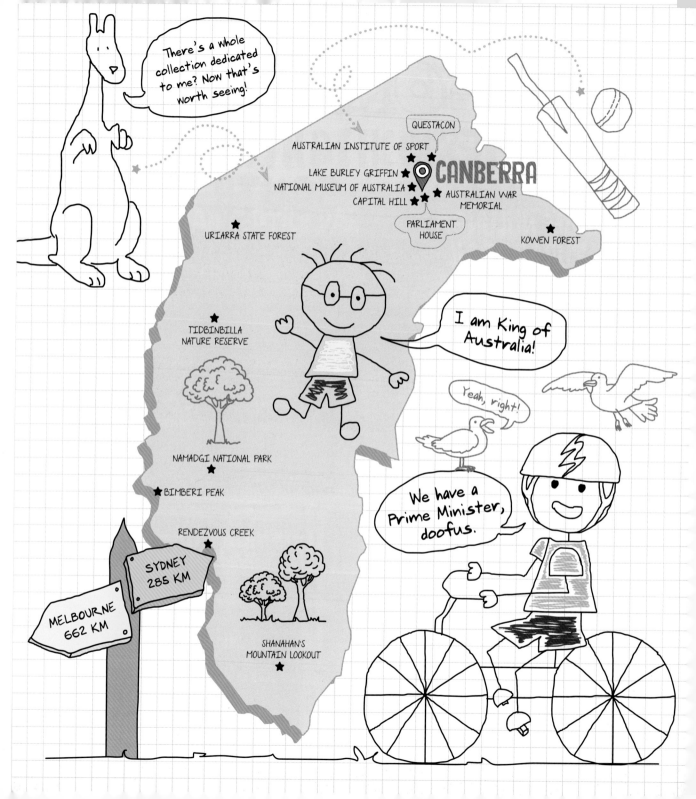

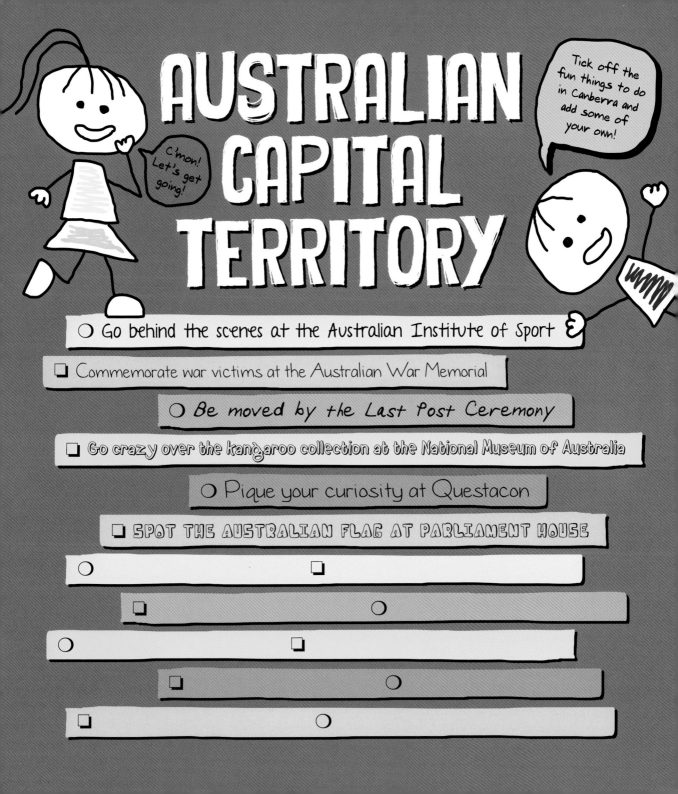

TOP SPOTS

CANBERRA

Australian Institute of Sport

Australia is a sport-crazy nation. Even as far back as 1894, it held its first national swimming championships. So when Australia performed badly at the 1976 Montreal Olympic Games, the nation took it hard. Australia came 32nd overall, taking home just one silver and four bronze medals. One newspaper called the event the 'Goldless Games'. Soon after, the idea for a sports training institute sprang into action.

SPORTS SCENE

You can go behind the scenes to see where Australia's sporting elite train. Better still, one of the athletes will be your tour guide.

FUN FACTOR

Sportex is an interactive sports experience where you can have a go at wheelchair basketball, virtual downhill skiing, rock climbing and much more.

Australian War Memorial

In Australia in the 1960s, 20-year-old men had to register for the National Service Scheme. If their birth date was drawn from a ballot, there was a chance they would be required to fight in the Vietnam War. The Australian War Memorial is a moving museum that recounts historical events like this and commemorates more than 100,000 Australians who have sacrificed their lives during wars. It's filled with war machines, weapons, records and relics that explore Australia's wartime history. There are many hands-on displays, including a World War I trench and an Iroquois helicopter, which was the workhorse of the air during the Vietnam War.

PIPER FAREWELL

The last post is a military call played on a bugle that lets soldiers know it's time to retire for the night. Museum visitors are given a similar farewell every day (except Christmas Day) at 4.55pm during the Last Post Ceremony. At each ceremony, a story behind a man or woman who was killed in war is read out. Each year, 364 stories are told.

POIGNANT PINE

There's a special tree at the museum known as Lone Pine. It was raised from a pine cone found on Lone Pine ridge at Gallipoli. During World War I, a soldier sent the cone to his mother. He and his brother had taken part in a battle at Gallipoli in which his brother was killed in action. Their mother raised the pine tree and presented it to the War Memorial.

ART & WAR

The museum is full of war paintings. Wartime artists captured Australia's involvement during many of its conflicts.

SELFIE SPOT
The *Simpson and His Donkey* sculpture is a must-see. Take a selfie with these two World War I heroes.

EXPLORE MORE

CANBERRA

National Museum of Australia

This museum is home to hundreds of thousands of ordinary and rather extraordinary social history objects, including a letter written by the infamous Australian bush bandit Ned Kelly, the large heart of the champion racehorse Phar Lap and love tokens created by English convicts before they were transported to Australia to serve out their sentences.

I sure am popular!

Kangaroo collection

One collection will get kangaroo lovers jumping with joy. It is called Hopping Mad and has more than 150 kangaroo-inspired objects, including an 1885 ceramic kangaroo umbrella stand and a real kangaroo paw that is part of a cigar lighter!

Car of the nation

The first ever Holden prototype car is housed at the museum. The iconic Australian car almost received a very Australian name: Emu, Boomerang and Austral were considered as possible names!

WEIRD WILDLIFE
The museum has bottles of marsupial bodies and body parts, such as the digestive system of a koala!

Parliament House

What do you notice when you look at Parliament House? Is it the beautiful mosaic in the forecourt? Is it the stunning design of the building? Or is it the flag flying proud? Well, you might almost miss the flag because it looks tiny, but, in fact, it's the size of a double-decker bus. That's not all that's remarkable about it. It isn't just one flag — there are 10 of them. Parliament is all about rules, and even the flag has to follow rules, such as it can't fly if it's damaged or faded. It's destroyed if it can't be repaired, and it must never touch the ground! That's one mean mission, because Parliament House has been open since 1988.

Concrete feat

So much concrete went into Parliament House's construction. There was enough to build 25 Sydney Opera Houses!

For sale

Sometimes, labour disputes took place on the building site. Once, during a plumbers' dispute, one person thought the project wouldn't go ahead, so he put an ad in the newspaper. He advertised the flag mast for sale!

Questacon

This national science and technology centre is so much fun it will get your heart racing — and when your heart rate does increase, you can see it as beats per minute on an LCD screen! With more than 200 hands-on exhibits, curiosity is the key here. You can make coloured shadows, use a 'shake table' to simulate an earthquake, and stand in a huge three-way mirror kaleidoscope to see your reflection repeated to infinity.

Robot power

The robot on display at the centre is named RoboQ. Have fun making this humanoid move, speak and sing.

Maybe I could sing on a talent show?

WHAT'S IN A NAME?

The name 'Questacon' is a combination of two words: 'quest' means to search or seek, and 'con' means to study or examine carefully.

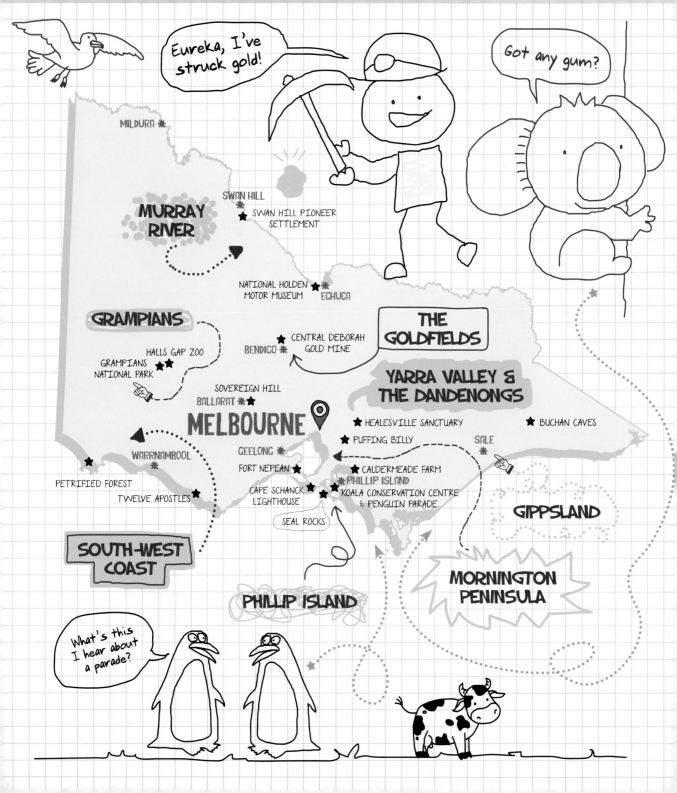

VICTORIA

> Maybe they should have called it Gotham ...

Best city

Melbourne is the capital of Victoria. In 2014, it was voted the WORLD'S most liveable city for the fourth year in a row.

Batman established MELBOURNE in 1835! It wasn't Batman the Caped Crusader though. It was an Australian farmer named John Batman who, along with a group of settlers from Tasmania, wanted extra land to raise his sheep. However, that same year, John Fawkner and another Tasmanian group also chose the area to establish a settlement. Therefore, both men claim to have founded Melbourne, and, not surprisingly, ended up bitter rivals (just like Batman and the Joker).

Oldest building

Cooks' Cottage is the oldest building in Australia. Originally, it was built in England in 1755 by the parents of explorer Captain James Cook. To make the journey to Melbourne in 1934, the cottage's bricks were dismantled, numbered, stored in barrels and transported by ship.

Hottest town

You'll be hot stuff in Mildura. That's because it has 77 days per year, on average, above 30°C. In 2014, it was Victoria's hottest town; the hottest day that year (14 January) was a sizzling 45.2°C.

Most cast iron

In the 1880s, Melbourne went cast-iron crazy! It now has more decorative cast iron than any other city around the globe. Cast-iron verandahs and balconies were all the rage and were known as 'iron petticoats'.

FUN FACTS

Quirkiest festival

The Victorian town of Merbein hosts an annual baking contest called the Great Australian Vanilla Slice Triumph. Step this way for the world's finest snot-blocks, folks!

Smallest & largest field

The Melbourne Cup horse race is known as 'the race that stops a nation'. In 1863, the smallest field, with just seven horses, took part in the race. In 1890, the largest field ever, with 39 horses, lined up at the start. Giddyup!

Largest tram network

Melbourne has the world's largest operating tram network with 250 kilometres of double tracks and 1763 tram stops.

Best invention

Professor Graeme Clark put Victoria on the map. He invented the bionic ear, aka the cochlear implant. He was inspired by a large seashell and a blade of grass!

That's something to roar about!

Melbourne Zoo

Melbourne Zoo is Australia's oldest zoo, established in 1862. In the early days, it used to be more of an entertainment venue with elephant rides and train rides. Visitors could even feed the animals. The zoo creatures were kept in old circus cages, then wooden houses, followed by brick enclosures with iron bars. Today, naturalistic exhibits imitate the wild. Lion Gorge, for instance, is based on a savannah waterhole and has a real crocodile in the enclosure's pool!

ELEPHANT ANTICS

For 40 years up until 1944, Queenie the elephant used to take zoo visitors for rides. She'd often do about 500 rides a day.

HEALTH HAZARD

In the early 1900s, an orangutan named Mollie used to light up and smoke cigarettes at the zoo. Apart from being bad for her health, she would often set her hessian bedding alight! What we want to know is, who was giving her the ciggies?

ARTIFICIAL ANIMALS

Not all the animals at the zoo are real. There are 30 horses on the 1878 carousel, which arrived at the zoo in 1963. Twenty of the horses are English and ten are German.

Just call me Your Royal HIGHness!

FUN FACTOR
The zoo runs various 'Wild Encounters'. One lets you sleep the night in the Elephant House and is called Roar 'n' Snore!

Old Melbourne Gaol

Melbourne's oldest and most notorious prison has held 133 hangings. The most famous of them all was the hanging of outlaw Ned Kelly in 1880. The Kelly family was often in trouble. Ned's father was an Irish convict whose crime was stealing two pigs, and his mother was imprisoned in the women's section of the Old Melbourne Gaol while Ned waited to be hanged! Not all the prisoners in the jail were criminals though; it also housed the mentally ill and homeless.

YES, YOUR HONOUR

The Old Magistrates' Court is the perfect place to imagine a famous case. You can sit in the dock, the judge's seat or the public gallery.

PRISON LOCKUP

Watch out when the sergeant-in-charge is about. People visiting the Watch House can be arrested (not for real, of course) and locked up!

I didn't do it! I'm INNOCENT!

NASTY PAST-Y

Ned's skull was stolen from the jail in 1978. It resurfaced 30 years later. However, forensic scientists discovered it was never actually Ned's head! A death mask at the jail is Ned's though. It was made about an hour after he died.

37

Royal Botanic Gardens: The Ian Potter Foundation Children's Garden

When visiting the Royal Botanic Gardens, make sure you check out the Ian Potter Foundation Children's Garden here too. Explore the many different landscapes made out of plants and the water-play features. Spaces include a bamboo forest, a tea-tree tunnel, fun fountains, a kitchen garden and an Indigenous garden. Let your imagination run wild as you splash, climb, hide, build and dig.

WATERY WONDERLAND

Water-play features, such as jumping fountains and the rill (a stream), are a great way to cool down on hot days, so remember to pack your bathers!

I dig this place!

FUN FACTOR
Climb up the Tree Tower and spy on the children's garden from above.

Scienceworks

This attraction is a real kid magnet. In fact, it is the place to see magnets in action, along with other scientific equipment and principles. With the Lightning Room for a name, you know what happens in that theatre will be electrifying. Watch as a presenter simulates real lightning and produces 3-metre lightning bolts. Be amazed when a cloud is produced in a bottle and a pickle cucumber is made to glow!

STINKY BEGINNINGS

The museum is housed in the Spotswood Pumping Station, which processed sewage from 1898. Before that, horse droppings, human sewage and hospital waste used to flow in Melbourne's gutters and drains.

SCIENCE & STARS

Melbourne Planetarium is at Scienceworks. Relax in the reclining chairs below the 16-metre dome and be mesmerised by a space show.

FUN FACTOR
Try racing against Cathy Freeman, the famous Indigenous Australian sprinter. Ready, set, go!

EXPLORE MORE
MELBOURNE

Argh! My eyes are square!

Australian Centre for the Moving Image (ACMI)

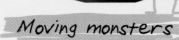

Adults won't tell you off for watching TV at ACMI, where film, television and digital culture are all celebrated. Located at Fed Square (see opposite), you can see everything from early film footage of the Melbourne Cup to the latest interactive video games. This is a place where your eyes might happily go square!

Moving monsters

'Screen Worlds' is ACMI's permanent exhibition, with loads of moving-image content and displays. One such display is 'Shadow Monsters', an interactive work where you move in front of a light-box to make your own scary monster. Boo!

Eureka Skydeck 88

The Eureka Stockade was an armed rebellion that took place on 3 December 1854 on the Ballarat goldfields. The Eureka Tower, which is Melbourne's tallest building, is named after this fiery battle. The tower has 92 storeys, and on the 88th floor is the observation deck, Eureka Skydeck 88. Live life on the edge by stepping into the glass cube that slides out from the building and is suspended 300 metres above the ground. Dare you to look down!

WHAT'S IN A NAME?
Many Chinese people believe the number 8 is lucky. Does that mean the Eureka Skydeck 88 is twice as lucky?

Up, up & away

The tower has 3680 steps. Luckily, it also has the fastest lifts in the Southern Hemisphere. The trip from the ground floor to level 88 takes only 38 seconds.

Federation Square

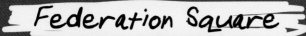

This iconic meeting place in Melbourne, built above a working railway, has had a colourful past. A city morgue, a fish market and railway yards have all called it home. Fed Square, as the locals call it, feels as if it has been part of the Melbourne cityscape for a long time. However, it only opened in 2002.

On time

The railway decking below Fed Square took a year to finish because the structural work could only be done in the wee hours of the morning during breaks in the train timetable.

Fed food

Fed Square's carpark roof is an edible garden. City residents can rent a veggie plot to grow their own food. Each plot is in a recycled apple crate.

I'm SO gonna find it first!

Let's go hunting!

WEIRD WILDLIFE
Fed Square has 467,000 sandstone cobblestones. Embedded in one cobblestone in the main square is a prehistoric oyster shell. Happy hunting!

Melbourne Aquarium

A 50-year-old mega creature (and a bit of a megastar) lives at the Melbourne Aquarium. He is one of the world's largest saltwater crocodiles in captivity, measuring a jaw-dropping 5 metres long. His name is Pinjarra, an Aboriginal word meaning 'place of soft grass and smooth water'. Pinjarra is not the only world-famous superstar at the aquarium. You can also see the world's only display of elephant sharks and the world's largest collection of seahorses and sea dragons.

Hey! We're hugely popular too! ... Much more entertaining than that cranky croc.

That smells fishy!

WEIRD WILDLIFE
The elephant shark has a trunk-like snout. Despite its name, it is not a true shark.

A bird's-eye view

In the glass cabins, you get a 360-degree view and commentary on what you're seeing. On a clear day, you can see about 40 kilometres into the distance.

Melbourne Star Observation Wheel

Ready to go for a spin — a very slow spin of 11 metres per minute? As high as a 40-storey building, the Melbourne Star is the only large observation wheel in the Southern Hemisphere and just one of four in the world. Its star design is based on the seven-point Federation of Australia star on the Australian flag. This giant wheel is strong: the steel alone is heavier than 3300 racehorses!

That looks wheely fun! Hehehe!

National Gallery of Victoria

AUSTRALIA'S FIRST PUBLIC ART GALLERY, the National Gallery of Victoria (NGV) has always been a popular destination. Founded in 1861, on Queen Victoria's birthday (24 May), the first exhibition was a right royal success. About 62,000 people came along, which was about 25 per cent of the colony's population. At that time, the art gallery was housed in the Victorian State Library. Today it occupies buildings in two different locations: NGV International is on St Kilda Rd on the edge of the city centre, while the Ian Potter Centre: NGV Australia is at Federation Square (see p.41). It is the most visited gallery in Australia.

Art robbers

In 1986, the NGV had plenty to weep about. Art thieves stole the famous painting *Weeping Woman* by Pablo Picasso. Two weeks later, NGV had tears of joy. The painting was found in a locker at a Melbourne railway station!

NASTY PAST-Y

In 1940, the gallery paid a tidy sum for a painting entitled *Head of a Man* that was thought to be by Vincent van Gogh. Unfortunately, it turned out that the famous Dutch artist hadn't actually painted it! Ooops!

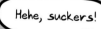
Hehe, suckers!

Shrine of Remembrance

The best time to visit the Shrine of Remembrance is at **11AM ON 11 NOVEMBER**. That's when a ray of sunlight goes through an aperture in the shrine's ceiling and falls onto the Stone of Remembrance, lighting up the word 'love'. This special time in November is the anniversary of the Armistice, which was signed in 1918 and marked the end of hostilities on the Western Front during World War I. Don't worry if you can't visit on that one special day of the year though. The 'Ceremony of Light' is performed every 30 minutes with electric light!

Hummm! It's 10.59!

On guard

Since 1935, guards have protected the shrine. Back then, 250 Victoria police members wanted to become shrine guards, but only 12 of them were selected. They were all highly decorated veterans who had fought in World War I.

Father & son

In the Crypt is a special sculpture entitled *Father & Son*. The father honours those who served in World War I and the son honours those who fought in World War II. Sometimes, fathers and sons fought in the same war.

DID YOU KNOW ...
The Shrine was built to commemorate Australians who fought in World War I and the 19,000 Victorians who died in the war.

Werribee Open Range Zoo

Africa meets Australia at the Werribee Open Range Zoo. Animals of the African savannahs and wetlands have plenty of space to roam. A safari bus allows visitors to go off-road and to get up close to animals such as zebras, giraffes, rhinos and ostriches. Australian animals also enjoy the wide, open spaces. Originally, the zoo took in surplus animals from Melbourne Zoo (see p. 36).

Hey, I'm here too! And I'm prettier than a giraffe!

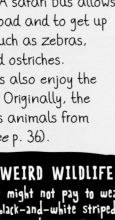

WEIRD WILDLIFE
It might not pay to wear black-and-white striped clothes to the zoo. Zebras are attracted to that pattern!

Yarra Bend Park

Yarra Bend Park is peaceful and tranquil today, however, it hasn't always been like that. Machine-gun practice during World War II took place at the cliffs near Deep Rock. A hospital for infectious diseases and a women's prison were set up in the park in 1904 and 1956 respectively. There was also a mental asylum here between 1848 and 1925. By all accounts patients weren't treated too well: for instance, 28 inmates were forced to share the same bath water!

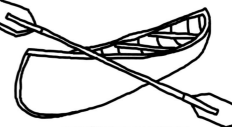

Paddle in the park

Head to the Studley Park Boathouse located within Yarra Bend Park and get paddling! You can hire canoes, kayaks and rowboats.

River record

The Studley Park Boathouse is the oldest public boathouse on the Yarra River. It was built in 1863 by the Burn family and was originally named Riversdale.

EXPLORE MORE
MORNINGTON PENINSULA

Gee, I wouldn't mind some chips!

CAPE SCHANCK LIGHTHOUSE

Whale-oil burners kept the Cape Schanck lighthouse blazing from 1859 when it first became operational. Luckily for the whales, kerosene burners and then an electric motor took over the job of powering the lamp. This lighthouse is one of Australia's oldest. Today, visitors can glimpse into the life of a lighthouse keeper at Cape Schanck in the olden days. Back then, the keepers had to manually wind the clock mechanism that rotated the lamp every hour of every day of every year. They must have been good at catnapping!

FORT NEPEAN

Did you know that the first shot fired by the Allied troops in World War I didn't happen in Europe? It actually took place at Fort Nepean on the Mornington Peninsula at 12.45pm on 5 August 1914. Australian troops fired across the bow of the German cargo steamer SS *Pfalz* as it attempted to slip out of Australian waters. Today, Fort Nepean still has barracks tunnels, gun emplacements, ammunition magazines, an engine house and a bomb-proof room.

That's some super cool stuff!

NASTY PAST-Y
A duel took place nearby in 1843. Two early settlers shot at each other. There was one casualty – a poor seagull flying past!

Bird brains!

SAFETY & SECURITY
The fort had shells, fuses and gunpowder, so on-duty artillerymen had to take off their clothing and hobnailed boots and put on working overalls and canvas shoes. They also removed metal and matches from their pockets. Sparks were the enemy!

OLD SO SOLD
In 1948 after the end of World War II, some guns at Point Nepean were sold for scrap. Luckily, some were found and retrieved for their historical importance.

48

EXPLORE MORE
PHILLIP ISLAND

Time for a little nap.

KOALA CONSERVATION CENTRE

With the security of a fence protecting them from possible dangers, the koalas at the Koala Conservation Centre can get on with what they do best — sleeping and eating. They sleep for up to 22 hours a day and eat eucalyptus leaves, which are highly poisonous to most other animals. Treetop boardwalks allow visitors to see koalas up close as these furry creatures snack and snooze the day away.

PENGUIN PARADE

Sunset means action on Phillip Island. That's when one of the largest penguin colonies in Australia waddles its way across the beach to the safety of the penguins' nest burrows. Since 1968, rangers have counted the penguins as they come ashore. Hundreds of visitors also come nightly to watch the little penguins, the smallest of the 17 kinds of penguins.

SEAL ROCKS

A group of small rocky islands off the coast of Phillip Island has a strong smell of wet seal fur and seal poop! Scientists are regular visitors to the islands, which are home to one of Australia's largest Australian fur seal populations. However, the scientists don't visit during the breeding season for fear of causing the adults, which are scared of humans, to stampede and harm the seal pups. Tourists also study the fur seals, but at a safe distance on seal-watching cruises.

You can count on us!

49

EXPLORE MORE
YARRA VALLEY & THE DANDENONGS

Hey! I'm NOT a duck!

HEALESVILLE SANCTUARY

From platypuses that like their tummies tickled to parrots and birds of prey, Healesville Sanctuary, a zoo that specialises in native Australian animals, has many furry and feathered friends. The wildlife hospital here treats more than 2000 injured or sick native animals each year; it might not be for the faint-hearted though, because visitors get to watch real surgery!

WEIRD WILDLIFE
Platypuses are sometimes known as duckbills, because their snout looks like a duck's bill.

PUFFING BILLY

Puffing Billy, a well-known and well-loved steam train, first puffed its way onto the scene in the early 1900s. Its purpose was to transport early settlers in the Dandenong Ranges to Melbourne so they could sell their produce. In 1953, a landslide closed Puffing Billy's line, but luckily, the Puffing Billy Preservation Society established itself in 1955. It went on to save the train, so Puffing Billy is still choof-choofing away today.

FIRE, FIRE!
On fire-danger days, fire-patrol vehicles travel behind Puffing Billy so that any fires can be detected, reported and extinguished.

THE GREAT TRAIN RACE
The Great Train Race has Puffing Billy really puffing – as well as up to 3500 runners. Every year, runners race against Puffing Billy, and many beat the train.

QUICK!

EXPLORE MORE
GRAMPIANS

That sounds like fun!

GRAMPIANS NATIONAL PARK

This 168,000 hectares of sandstone mountains, waterfalls, animals and wildflowers is perfect for camping, rock climbing and bushwalking. It is a weather buff's dream location, because in this area the year is divided into six different weather cycles or seasons. For culture vultures, there are more than 200 ancient Aboriginal rock-art sites.

STARTING POINT

Brambuk the National Park & Cultural Centre is a good place to find out all there is to see and do at Grampians National Park. You can even paint a boomerang there.

HALLS GAP ZOO

About 160 species of mammals, reptiles and birds wander, slither or fly at this 52-acre, open-setting wildlife zoo. Visitors can have a close encounter with residents such as an alligator, a snake, a chameleon, a dingo or a meerkat. Once, a female visitor had a rather too-close encounter when a snake ended up looped through her jeans like a belt!

WILDLIFE WELFARE

All native wildlife in Victoria is protected. It can't be killed, trapped, traded or held in captivity without a special permit.

Mmm. It's so nice to meet you. Is it lunchtime yet?

EXPLORE MORE
SOUTH-WEST COAST

PETRIFIED FOREST

Back in 1963, it was suggested that the Petrified Forest at Cape Bridgewater was a forest that was buried by an advancing sand dune. Since then it has been discovered that the 'fossil trees' are not moulds of buried tree trunks at all, but rather 'solution pipes', which form when acidic water solidifies the surrounding porous sand.

This is my petrified face!

SELFIE SPOT
Stand next to one of the hollow tubes and smile, but make sure only one of you looks petrified!

TWELVE APOSTLES

The Twelve Apostles are limestone sea stacks found east of Port Campbell on the Great Ocean Road. However, there aren't actually 12 stacks — even in the 1920s when they were named, there were only eight. Today, seven stacks remain. Sadly, the eighth one toppled into the ocean in 2005. Not to worry though: new stacks are constantly forming, so there may be 12 some time in the future!

PIG & PIGLETS

Up until 1922, the limestone stacks were called the Sow and Piglets. Muttonbird Island was the sow while the smaller rocks were all her piglets.

Awesome!

EXPLORE MORE
MURRAY RIVER

I've got more horse-power than any car!

NATIONAL HOLDEN MOTOR MUSEUM

In Australia, most petrol heads are either Holden fans or Ford enthusiasts. Of course, at the Holden Museum in Echuca, they love their Holdens. The Holden FX, the all-Australian car, rolled along in 1948. It was a real Aussie icon alongside meat pies, kangaroos and gum trees! At the museum, more than 40 cars are on display, including the famous millionth car, the 1962 EJ Holden.

EQUESTRIAN ERA

James Holden's business opened in 1856, but back then it produced horse saddles, not cars. How times change!

SWAN HILL PIONEER SETTLEMENT

One of the stars at the Swan Hill Pioneer Settlement is the paddle-steamer *Gem*. Nicknamed the 'Queen of the Murray', *Gem* travelled on the Murray River from 1876 as a barge, then as a passenger-cargo carrier from 1882. To get ready for carrying passengers, *Gem* had an extreme makeover. She was cut in half and pulled apart by bullocks so that a middle section could be added to make her bigger. The Pioneer Settlement has many other objects from Australia's pioneering days, including replica carriages and original and replica heritage buildings. If only their walls could talk!

STORIES OF THE PAST

During the Sound & Light show after sunset, the buildings do talk! Visitors ride in a vehicle past the buildings. One by one, the buildings light up and voices tell stories from the past.

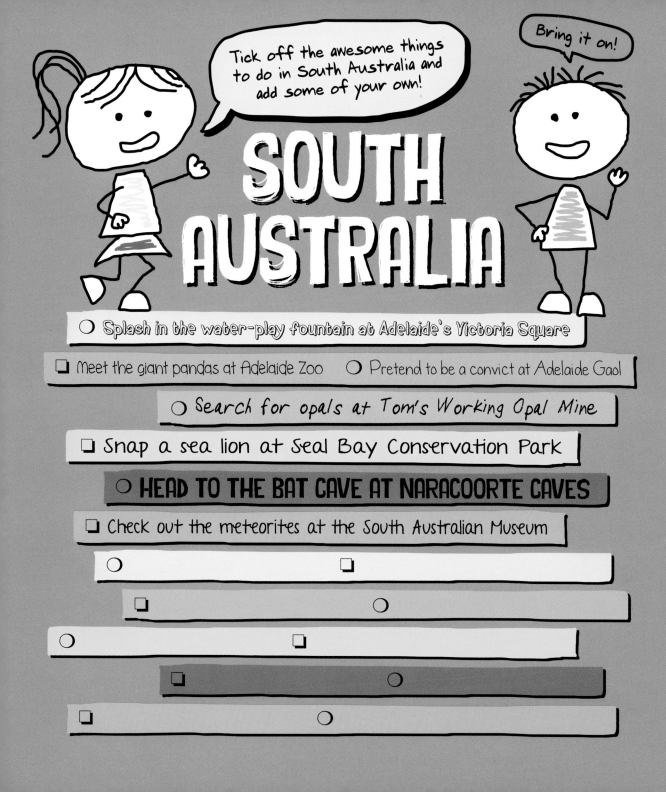

Sweet!

SOUTH AUSTRALIA

Oldest flamingo

In 2014, the oldest resident of Adelaide Zoo and the oldest flamingo in the world sadly died. The famous bird was aged 83!

The city of **ADELAIDE** is the capital of South Australia and is named after German-born Queen Adelaide, wife of King William IV of England. In 1836, the city's founder, Colonel William Light, had the task of finding suitable land for the new colony. He had to be quick about it though, because the first free settlers began to arrive later that same year. In his 1837 city plan, he imagined Victoria Sq to be a vibrant public space for Adelaide, however, it was still a dusty paddock until 1854!

Most dangerous coast

Be careful when sailing around South Australia. There are more than 80 shipwrecks around Kangaroo Island alone (and that's just since 1836)!

Hottest place

Australia's hottest recorded temperature was reached in Oodnadatta in 1960, when the mercury in a thermometer climbed to 50.7°C. Wonder if anyone tried frying an egg on a car bonnet that day?

Urgh, it's soooooooo hot.

FUN FACTS

Oldest prison

Adelaide Gaol closed in 1988. It was the longest continuously operating prison in Australia. Its other claim to fame is it is one of the two oldest public buildings in South Australia.

longest place name

Mamungkukumpurangkuntjunya Hill is the longest official place name in South Australia (as well as the whole of Australia). With a whopping 30 letters, the Pitjantjatjara Aboriginal name means 'where the devil urinates'.

Oldest chocolate maker

The oldest family owned chocolate maker in Australia is Haigh's Chocolates. The first store opened in 1915 on King William St in Adelaide.

largest urban park

Adelaide Park Lands is Australia's largest urban park. It is a whopping 930 hectares. What's even more impressive is that it has about 350,000 trees!

South Australian Maritime Museum

As soon as you step inside here, it's pretty obvious you've walked into a maritime museum. The clue? A replica ketch named *Active II* sits proudly in the entrance gallery. Many ask how such a big vessel squeezed into the museum, but the answer remains a secret! The relatively young museum opened in 1986, showcasing an inherited collection (the oldest nautical collection in the Southern Hemisphere). It features shipwreck artefacts, nautical instruments, figureheads, paintings, model ships and even swimming costumes.

BODIES ON THE BOW

Figureheads are sculptures that were placed on the bow of a sailing vessel. The museum has 17 of them, which is the largest collection in the Southern Hemisphere. Popular figureheads included swans, lions and naked women. During the French Revolution, one vessel had a guillotine as its figurehead!

Ahoy!

Polly wants a cracker!

SHIPWRECK!

The museum's exhibition on shipwrecks is appropriately named 'Wrecked! Tragedy and the Southern Seas'. South Australia has a long history of maritime disasters; there are a staggering 850 shipwrecks along its coastline.

SELFIE SPOT
'Museum Selfie Day' takes place around the world in January. Look up the exact date on Twitter, because it changes every year. Post a picture of you at the Maritime Museum and use the hashtag #museumselfie.

PORT ADELAIDE

The museum is in the heart of Port Adelaide. In 1836, not everyone was thrilled about Port Adelaide's original landing place. It was a swamp plagued by mosquitoes and bad weather. That's why it received the nickname Port Misery!

South Australian Museum

In 1883, the curator of this museum tried to get rid of its original name, the South Australian Institute Museum, because he thought it wasn't 'particularly handsome'. The request was finally actioned more than 55 years later. Luckily, the museum is packed full of particularly handsome and interesting objects, such as a 17-metre-long whale skeleton, an ancient Egyptian mummy and polar explorer Sir Douglas Mawson's camelhair sleeping bag!

WEIRD WILDLIFE
The largest ammonite (marine fossil) ever discovered in Australia is housed at the museum. At first, it was believed to be a dumped tyre!

It's called camouflage, people!

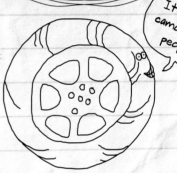

REWARD!

There are about 150 meteorites at the museum, including two from Mars. Keep your eyes peeled when you're exploring Australia, because the museum offers a reward for any meteorite finds.

MAWSON MEMORABILIA

Frank Hurley took the now-famous photo of Douglas Mawson wearing a balaclava. The woolen headgear was donated to the museum in 2010. In the photo, Mawson's balaclava is inside out!

There's heaps of cool stuff here!

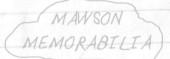

EXPLORE MORE

ADELAIDE

Adelaide Oval

The Adelaide Oval has been the home of South Australian cricket since the 1870s. It's also been the venue for tennis and football matches, royal visits, rock concerts, carnivals, air-raid demonstrations and Highland Games. But perhaps the most spectacular event happened on 13 October 1915. To entertain the crowd at a special event, two trams took part in a choreographed crash, which saw them burst into flames!

Whoops!

Famous scoreboard

A manual scoreboard, erected in 1911, still stands at the oval. At the end of a football game in 1928, the crowd went wild, not because their favourite team had won, but because an attendant had added up the score on the scoreboard incorrectly. The game was, in fact, a draw.

Cricket legend

Australian batsman Sir Donald Bradman was one of the world's greatest cricketers. His personal collection of cricket memorabilia is at the Adelaide Oval.

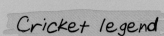

NASTY PAST-Y

In 1895, female cricket-club members were required to sit in a separate area of the members' stand. Talk about discrimination!

Migration Museum

The Migration Museum is housed in what was once the Destitute Asylum, which shut its doors in 1918. Wander around Settlement Sq to view the pavers that have the names, origins and arrival dates of some of the immigrants who settled in South Australia.

SELFIE SPOT

The Immigrants statue stands by Settlement Sq. Snap a selfie while you help the father carry the family's suitcase!

Victoria Square

What would Adelaide's founder, William Light, have thought about Victoria Sq having an urban lounge and a water-play fountain? The square was intended to be the hub of the city. The name Light wrote on his plan was 'the Great Square', but it ended up being named after Queen Victoria of England. The unveiling of her statue occurred on 11 August 1894 at 4pm. This time was chosen because it didn't interfere with any football game or horserace!

Mourning statue

When Queen Victoria died in 1901, her statue was covered in black, which is the colour of mourning in many countries.

Am I interrupting something?

EXPLORE MORE
MOUNT GAMBIER & LIMESTONE COAST

ADMELLA DISCOVERY TRAIL

Picture this: the SS *Admella* hits Carpenters Reef on 6 August 1859. The passengers and crew cling to the wreck as towering waves try to swallow them up. With little food or fresh water, some people drink salty seawater and are driven mad; others are swept away, never to be seen again. On day eight, rescuers finally manage to get to the survivors. Sadly, of the 113 people aboard, 89 lose their lives.

THE TAIL TRAIL

Follow the 21 trail markers (within a 130-kilometre radius of Mount Gambier) that recount the tale of the SS *Admella* disaster.

WHAT'S IN A NAME?
SS *Admella* was named after three of the ship's trading ports:
AD Adelaide
MEL Melbourne
LA Launceston

NARACOORTE CAVES

For 500,000 years, unsuspecting animals fell into the Naracoorte Caves and perished when they discovered they couldn't climb out. It wasn't just a few animals that ended their days in these death traps. Tens of thousands of fossil bones have been unearthed in the Victoria Fossil Cave alone. The bones came from 118 different animals, some of which are now extinct.

BABY BATS

The Bat Cave is just one of two known maternity caves for the critically endangered southern bent-wing bat. In summer at dusk, you can watch the bats fly from the Bat Cave to hunt for insects.

UMPHERSTON SINKHOLE

A sunken garden grows in this sinkhole, which formed when the roof of a limestone cave collapsed onto the cave floor. In the 1860s, James Umpherston became the owner of the sinkhole, which was located on a property he purchased. In about 1886, he established a garden in the giant hole and carved a path in the side of the rock. When he died in 1900, the garden filled up with weeds and remained overgrown for the next 75 years, when it was restored.

BOAT RIDES

There was once a lake in the sinkhole. James Umpherston arranged for visitors to go for boat rides.

SNACK SPOT

When darkness falls, locals come armed with fruit and bread to feed the resident possums.

That's pretty neat!

EXPLORE MORE

COOBER PEDY & THE OUTBACK

OLD TIMERS MINE

Old Timers Mine was sealed up in 1916. No-one really knows who hid the mine that was dug by hand, or why. The first anyone knew of its existence was in 1968 when a local, Ron Gough, was doing work on his underground home in Coober Pedy (it gets so hot here, people live below the ground!). He was working on an extension to his house, when suddenly he broke through to the concealed mine. With its three seams of opal, he had quite literally stumbled upon a goldmine — but with opals!

OPAL FINDS

A 14-year-old boy named William Hutchison found the first opals at Coober Pedy. It was 1 February 1915, and he was searching for fresh water at the time (while searching for gold), but found opals on the ground instead. Happy days!

WHAT'S IN A NAME?
Coober Pedy, the opal capital of the world, is derived from the Aboriginal words 'kupa piti', which mean 'white man in a hole'.

Opals, opals everywhere!

WARNING! WARNING!

Open opal shafts can be dangerous. People and even cars have fallen into abandoned shafts.

DANGER

DON'T RUN   BEWARE!   DON'T WALK BACKWARDS

DEEP SHAFTS

UNMARKED HOLES

Even I'm faster!

OUTBACK MAIL RUN

Twice a week, a special mail person sets out from Coober Pedy on a 600-kilometre journey to deliver post to the remote outposts of South Australia. One of the stops is the biggest cattle station in the world, Anna Creek Station, which is about the size of Belgium! Located in the middle of the station is William Creek, South Australia's smallest town. A very cool adventure is to tag along with the postie on a tour.

ROOM TO ROAM

There's plenty of room to roam in the outback and it takes plenty of time. The outback mail run tour works on bush time and can take up to 12 hours. Talk about snail mail!

TOM'S WORKING OPAL MINE

Enjoy the fun of this working opal mine in Coober Pedy. Ride on a bosun's chair, which is a piece of timber fixed to a hook on a winch cable. Use divining rods to locate an opal seam. Or try your hand at noodling, which is a term used to describe searching for opals in discarded mining materials.

BUZZ OFF!

Flies plague Coober Pedy. It's a welcome relief to go underground into a fly-free zone.

Blasted flies!

EXPLORE MORE
KANGAROO ISLAND

KANGAROO ISLAND

In 1802, when explorer Captain Matthew Flinders spotted mobs of kangaroos on this large island off the South Australian coast, he knew exactly what to call it — Kangaroo Island, of course! Some of the island's place names have gory stories behind them: Stink Corner got its name because a man used to discard wallaby carcasses there!

ISLAND INHABITANTS

About 2000 years ago, Aboriginal people lived on the island, but later abandoned it. Mainland Aboriginal people refer to the island as 'Karta', which means 'Land of the Dead'. Today, the locals call the island 'KI' for short.

LAID-BACK KANGAROOS

The kangaroo species on the island is unique. They are the slowest of all kangaroos because they have no natural predators, given the island's isolation.

WILD PLACE NAMES

The island is a wildlife haven. This is reflected in some of the place names, such as Emu Bay, Snake Lagoon, Seal Bay, Pelican Lagoon, Cygnet River, Cuttlefish Bay, Dolphin Cove, Snapper Point and Billygoat Falls. Don't forget your camera!

SANDBOARDING

When you've seen enough kangaroos, try sandboarding down the Little Sahara sand dunes.

FUN FACTOR

With 509 kilometres of coastline, Kangaroo Island is Australia's third largest island. That means there's plenty of space to run, swim — and hop!

Hop on over!

Kangaroos aren't the only animals who live here!

SEAL BAY CONSERVATION PARK

Some of the Kangaroo Island locals are sea lions. Seal Bay is home to the third biggest colony of Australian sea lions, which are found only in Australia. The sea lions might look lazy as they lounge about sunning themselves, however, they're usually having a well-deserved rest. These blubbery beasts can dive up to 1200 times on three-day hunting trips, taking few breaks.

I broke my diving record!

Only by a whisker!

SNAP A SEA LION

Scientists have thought of a novel way of tracking Australian sea lions. They want people to take photos (from a safe distance of about 20 metres) of the sea lions' snouts. The aim is to find out whether individual sea lions can be identified by their whisker spot patterns. If you're able to snap a sea lion, you can upload your picture via www.whiskerpatrol.org.

SNAZZY SEALERS

In the 1800s, sealers almost hunted the seals on Kangaroo Island to extinction. In 1817, the *Sydney Gazette* reported that the sealers 'dress in kangaroo skins without linen, and wear sandals made of sealskin. They smell like foxes'!

NASTY PAST-Y
During the sealing days of the 1800s, the beaches on Kangaroo Island were red from seal blood.

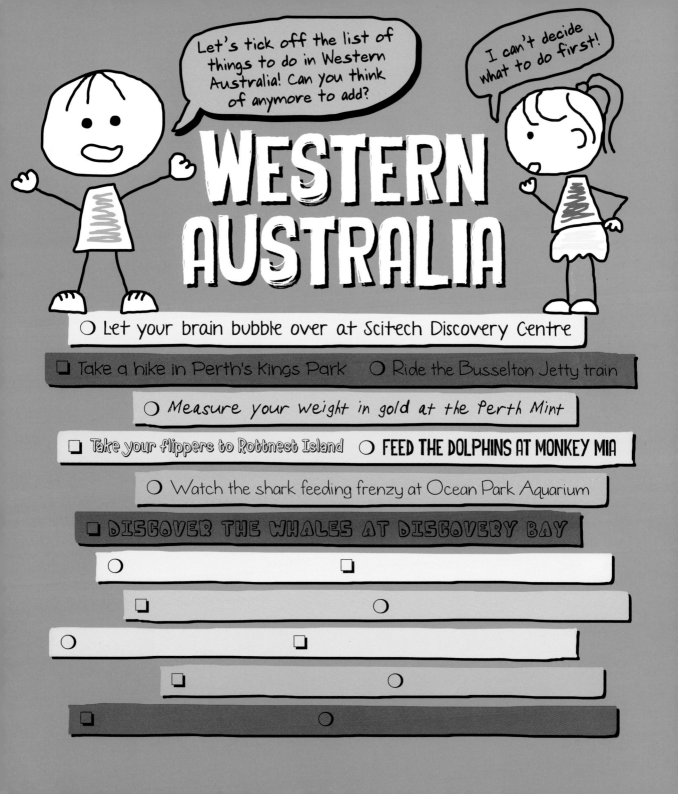

WILD!

WESTERN AUSTRALIA

Most sunny

Perth is Australia's **SUNNiEST** capital city. It is also one of the world's windiest. The 'Fremantle Doctor' is an iconic sea breeze that blows inland late in the day, cooling everything down.

Ships often have bottles of champagne smashed against them to celebrate their first launch. But to mark **PERTH**'s foundation in 1829, an axe was smashed against a tree. The tree was near where the Perth Town Hall now stands, and the ceremony symbolised the building of a new town. By 1962, Perth was smashing its way into world headlines. On 20 February of that year, an astronaut named John Glenn became the first American to orbit Earth. The city of Perth wanted to stand out and to acknowledge Glenn's achievement, so its residents switched on all their lights. Sure enough, Glenn reported seeing the city's lights as he flew over, and Perth has been nicknamed the 'City of Light' ever since!

Most isolated

Perth is the state capital of Western Australia, and Australia's most isolated capital city. It's also one of the most isolated capital cities in the world!

Longest place name

The longest name of a place near Perth is Ngangaguringguring Hill.

Try saying that 10 times, fast!

FUN FACTS

Largest inner-city park

Spreading over 400 hectares, Kings Park is Perth's largest inner-city park and its most visited park. It is also one of the largest inner-city parks in the world.

Oldest mint

Perth has Australia's oldest operating mint. Its most popular coins are the ones in the Australian animals theme set.

Most challenging road

Gibb River Road is a 660-kilometre dirt track in the Kimberley region. This road is so challenging that some vehicle manufacturers test their four-wheel-drive vehicles on it and then proudly boast 'Capable of handling the Gibb River Road' about the cars that pass the test.

FUUUN!

Best beach

Cable Beach near Broome is super popular with locals, visitors and even saltwater crocodiles. In February 2014, a large croc decided to take a dip, which caused quite a commotion. Luckily, there were plenty of places for people to hide on the 22-kilometre-long beach.

First street waterslide

On 14 December 2014, people slipped and slid down the first street waterslide in Australia. Located in Perth's St George's Tce, the slide was 315 metres long.

TOP SPOTS

PERTH

Kings Park

Thousands of trees call Kings Park home, and some have gone to great lengths to be there. In 2008, a giant 750-year-old boab tree, named Gija Jumulu, travelled more than 3200 kilometres. Its five-day journey caused quite a stir. Onlookers waved and sounded horns as police escorts made sure the tree arrived safely. Other things in the park command just as much attention, including large replicas of extinct Australian megafauna, an interactive water-misting forest and a tower shaped like a DNA molecule!

DUCK!

In 1862, convicts set to work and built a rifle range (along Fraser Ave) for the park's volunteer guards. In 1886, it closed for several months because people were complaining of stray bullets! (There's no need to worry about bullets these days though – the rifle range closed down completely in 1895.)

TREE PLANTING

The first tree planted was a Norfolk Island pine. The year was 1895.

This place is bloomin' nice!

WHAT'S IN A NAME?

In 1895, the park was given the name 'Perth Park'. Then, in 1901, when King Edward VII ascended the throne, the park was renamed 'the King's Park'.

74

Perth Mint

The Perth Mint can thank Coolgardie and Kalgoorlie for its existence. It first opened its doors in 1899 after gold was discovered in these towns, and gold diggers were soon depositing their findings. The first coin produced was an 1899 gold sovereign stamped with the mint mark 'P' (for Perth). Today, coins made here are sometimes weird and wonderful, and have included a glow-in-the-dark coin, a locket coin and a coin in the shape of Australia!

GOOD AS GOLD

Do you know the saying 'worth your weight in gold'? Well, you can literally find out your weight in gold at the Perth Mint – simply step on the special scales!

UNIQUE MESSAGE

Visitors can design a medallion with their own special message. An engraving machine carves the message into the metal.

GOLD POUR

You can watch a gold bar being poured at the mint. This happens seven times a day for the benefit of visitors. It's the same gold bar that gets melted and poured every time. So far, the gold has been used more than 36,000 times!

Yeah, well, I'm a good-looking bird.

WEIRD WILDLIFE
Between 2002 and 2005, Perth Mint produced square-shaped kookaburra coins.

75

Perth Zoo

In the zoo's early days, visitors were entertained not just by the animals. There were mineral baths, tennis tournaments, fashion parades, animal rides and even cute-baby contests. The first animals to live in the zoo were two monkeys, four ostriches, two lions, a tiger and an orangutan. Today, numbers have increased substantially: about 1300 animals now call Perth Zoo home.

SNACK SPOT
In the past, the zoo grew crops, such as lettuce, carrots and alfalfa, for the animals. What the animals didn't need was then sold to the residents of Perth!

Just hangin' around!

EARLY HOMES
In the zoo's first years, exhibits included two bear caves, a monkey house and a model castle for the guinea pigs!

Scitech Discovery Centre

You may think that science is not mind-blowing, but Scitech will soon change your mind. It's a hands-on interactive centre that will get your brain bubbling over as you explore concepts in science, technology, mathematics and engineering. Yes, really — these things can be fun!

DISCOVERY ZONE
The exhibits change but one thing remains constant – the fun factor. Scitech is like a cross between a science museum and a theme park!

The Bell Tower

This popular tourist attraction on the Swan River was built especially to house some bells — but not just any old bells. These Georgian ones had lived a colourful life for hundreds of years in the St Martin-in-the-Fields church in London's Trafalgar Sq. They had rung out when England won famous battles and during the coronations of many British monarchs. When they'd become too heavy for the church's foundations, there was talk of melting them down to make new bells. Luckily for Perth, a man from Australia stepped in and saved them and they were gifted to Western Australia to commemorate the 1988 bicentenary. There was just one small problem: the bells had to wait about 12 years for the Bell Tower to be built and opened!

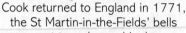

WELCOME HOME

When navigator Captain James Cook returned to England in 1771, the St Martin-in-the-Fields' bells rang out to welcome him home.

RHYME & CHIME

The old English nursery rhyme 'Oranges and Lemons' mentions the bells of St Martin-in-the-Fields, not just the bells of St Clement's!

BELL NAME

The largest of the bells is Zachariah. It is named after Reverend Zachariah Pearce, the vicar of St Martin-in-the-Fields in 1725.

SELFIE SPOT

Take a photo with the Bell Tower, one of the largest musical instruments in the world. That's something to chime about!

EXPLORE MORE

PERTH

Penguin Island

Just south of Perth, Penguin Island is home to penguins — no surprises there — but it also used to be home to an eccentric fellow who called himself 'King of Penguin Island'. Seaforth McKenzie came to the island in 1914 and set about creating a holiday resort, which operated up until 1926. He carved out tourist accommodation, a library and a shop in some limestone caves. Today, the island is a nature reserve, and not much evidence of the 'king's' reign remains.

WEIRD WILDLIFE

Little penguins are colourful creatures. They are bluish-grey and white, with a black bill, silvery-grey eyes and light-pink feet. The adults are the only penguins that do not have black-and-white feathers. They're energetic little things, swimming all day to catch fish and only coming ashore at dusk.

Largest & smallest

The island has Western Australia's largest colony of little penguins – the smallest penguin species in the world. About 1000 pairs nest there in winter.

That's some feat!

Rottnest Island

Like other islands in Australia in the 1800s, Rottnest Island hosted a prison and a boys' reformatory. However, from 1902, visitors started to explore Rottnest. Was that a problem? Not really, because the visitors were restricted to coming only on Sundays and the prisoners were kept well away from them during that time. From 1907, the penal settlement started to be turned into a holiday island. The prison and reformatory eventually became holiday hostels!

Breakaway island

About 7000 years ago, Rottnest Island separated from the mainland. It lies 19 kilometres off the coast of Fremantle.

A whole island just for us!

Blinding buildings

Long ago, the limestone buildings on the island were painted with whitewash, but the white colour was too harsh on the eyes in the bright sun. To make them ochre instead, rusty nails were added to the whitewash.

Flipper feet

The most useful footwear on the island may well be flippers. With 63 beaches and 20 bays, they are sure to come in handy.

WEIRD WILDLIFE

The Dutch explorer Willem de Vlamingh named the island Rottenest in 1696. The name means 'rat's nest'. He thought the native quokkas on the island were large rats!

EXPLORE MORE
THE SOUTH-WEST

BUSSELTON JETTY

Starting out life in 1865 at a mere 161 metres long, this jetty has been extended and extended … and extended some more! In fact, it has had nine extensions. Eight of them were in the late 1800s. Today, at 1841 metres in length (that's nearly 2 kilometres!), it is now the **LONGEST WOODEN-PILED JETTY** in the Southern Hemisphere. However, there have been events in its lifetime, such as a cyclone and a fire, that have caused the jetty to be temporarily shorter!

DAMAGE CONTROL

A cyclone swept through the area in 1978. About 700 metres of the oldest section ended up being destroyed, condemned and removed.

UNDER THE JETTY

At the end of the jetty is the Underwater Observatory, which goes 8 metres down to the ocean floor. It's a great place to spy on the 300 different kinds of things that live under the jetty.

FIRE, FIRE!

In 1999, a fire broke out on the jetty. About 70 metres of the structure burned. To contain the fire, firefighters cleverly chainsawed off the burning section so that it dropped into the sea, dousing the flames.

FUN FACTOR
Jump on the jetty train. Luckily, you can get a return ticket, or the walk back would make YOU huff and puff.

DISCOVERY BAY, ALBANY

You'll have a whale of a time here, but the whales in 1845 didn't. Back then, about 300 whale ships patrolled the surrounding waters to hunt them down. It took until 1963 before it became illegal to kill humpback whales in Australian waters. The Historic Whaling Station was the last operating whaling station in Australia. Today, you can see whale skeletons and go aboard a whale-chaser vessel. You can also watch presentations inside whale-oil storage tanks that have been transformed into theatres.

NATIVE CREATURES

Discovery Bay is not just about whales. There's also a native wildlife park here where you can get up close to koalas, wombats, possums, kangaroos, flying foxes and the like. Keep your eyes peeled for the rare white kangaroo too – it's a strain of the western grey kangaroo.

NASTY PAST-Y

Whales were caught, cut up and thrown into huge pressure cookers. They were caught for their oil, which was extracted from the cooked whale meat and used to fuel lamps.

Talk about BIG!

EXPLORE MORE
SHARK BAY

MONKEY MIA

Monkey Mia at Dolphin Beach in Shark Bay might be a bit of a mouthful, but it is well worth talking about. For more than 40 years, bottlenose dolphins have come to Monkey Mia to interact with people and be fed. The friendly dolphins visit almost every day. In fact, over the last five years, they've only missed four days. That's a pretty impressive attendance record!

DOLPHIN SAFETY

The dolphins' welfare is important. That's why it is advisable to not wear sunscreen on your hands and lower legs if you go into the water to interact with them. The sunscreen gets in the dolphins' eyes and stings them. Ouch!

Yeah, I'm pretty smart!

CLEVER CREATURES

The dolphins at Shark Bay have invented a unique fishing technique. They sometimes tear off sea sponges from the sea floor and put them on their beaks. This 'glove' protects them as they hunt among the sharp coral. They are the only dolphins on Earth to use tools to hunt.

WHAT'S IN A NAME?

The Monkey Mia dolphins have names. Some names are normal, such as Holly and Grant, while others are more unusual, like Crooked Fin and Hobbit. Two unfortunate dolphins ended up with the moniker 'No Name'!

There's room for one more!

OCEAN PARK AQUARIUM

An unsuspecting visitor might think that the sharks are the most terrifying creatures at Ocean Park Aquarium. However, there is something very deadly that looks very innocent — that is, if you can actually see it. The stonefish is an extremely poisonous fish that uses camouflage to ambush its prey. Its skin is textured like coral and rock, and it lies in wait among the rocks on the sea floor. Luckily at the aquarium, there are no such dangers, and with its rule of 'do not touch or feed the animals', you will be perfectly safe.

SHARK COUNT

At Shark Bay, there are at least 28 different kinds of sharks, but in the past 100 years, there have been no shark attacks.

FOOD FIGHT

Watch animals such as tiger sharks, lemon nurse sharks and nervous sharks get in a feeding frenzy during the feeding demonstrations. You'll see that there's nothing nervous about the nervous shark!

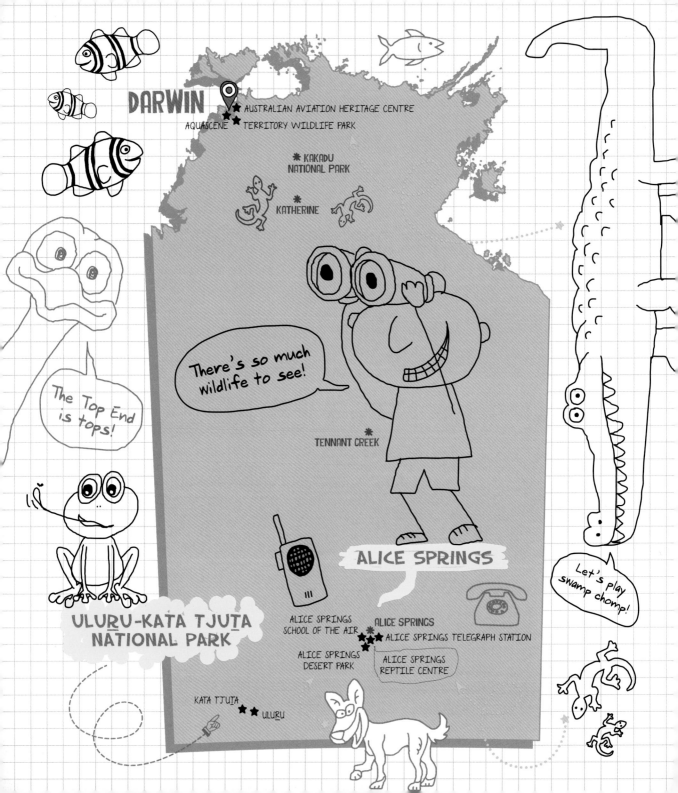

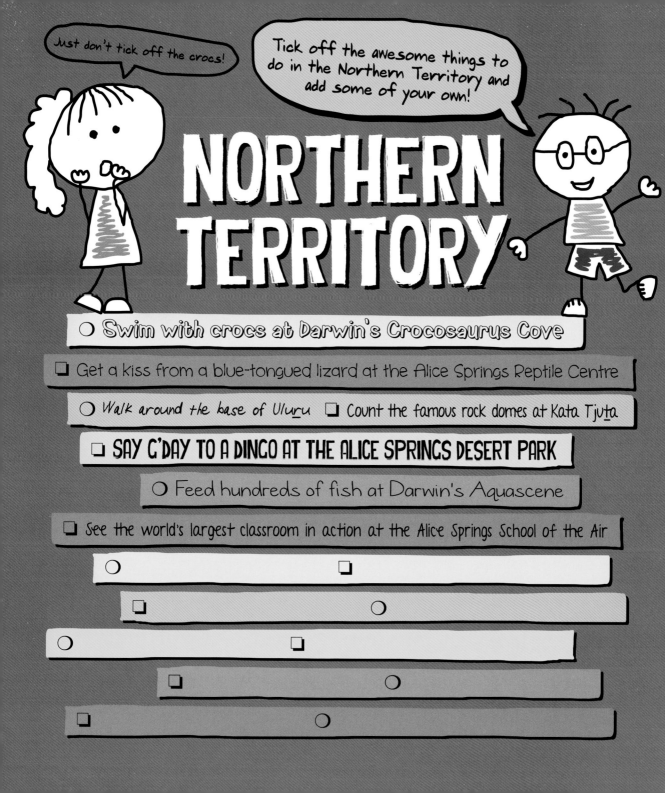

Awesome!

NORTHERN TERRITORY

Youngest city

Darwin has the youngest population of any capital city in Australia. The average age is about 33 years old. It is also Australia's smallest (by population) and most northerly capital city.

When you hear the city name 'DARWIN', you might immediately think of Charles Darwin, the famous British naturalist — and you would be right in your thinking. Darwin is the Northern Territory's largest city and its capital. It started off with the name Palmerston when it was established in 1869. However, by 1911, it was renamed in Charles Darwin's honour.

Most unusual waterfall

Now you see it, now you don't! Jim Jim Falls in Kakadu National Park look spectacular in the wet season, with water shooting down the 200-metre drop into a large pool below. But in the dry season, the falls disappear altogether!

Oldest building

The oldest remaining European building in Darwin and the Northern Territory is Government House. Construction of the original building took place in 1870. The building is a survivor: it has withstood cyclones, earthquakes, bombing raids and white ants!

First bombed

Darwin was the first place on mainland Australia to come under attack during World War II. On 19 February 1942, the Japanese raided Darwin from the air twice.

FUN FACTS

Most passengers

When Cyclone Tracy flattened much of Darwin in 1974, Qantas set a world record for carrying the most passengers on a plane. They evacuated 673 people onto a 747.

Longest taxi fare

The world's longest continuous taxi fare took place in 1930. An elderly woman asked a taxi driver to take her and her two friends from Victoria to Darwin and back. The journey of about 11,000 kilometres took place mainly on bush tracks. The amazing thing is they got only one puncture!

Largest croc

The record for the world's largest (and oldest) crocodile in captivity goes to Cassius, a saltie (saltwater crocodile) caught south of Darwin. He is fittingly named after the world-famous boxer Cassius Clay (aka Muhammad Ali).

I won't eat you. Well, maybe just a nibble ...

TOP SPOTS
DARWIN

Crocosaurus Cove

You wouldn't expect crocodiles to have an inner-city address, but they do here. At Crocosaurus Cove in the heart of Darwin, about 200 crocodiles eat, sleep — and snap! At this reptile retreat, visitors can swim with crocodiles, feed them and even hold them! Crocodiles are not the only attraction though. Crocosaurus Cove also has the largest collection of Australian reptiles on Earth.

WAX WORKS

The World of Crocs at Crocosaurus Cove is a bit like Madame Tussauds, but with crocs not humans. On display, there are 14 crocodilian wax replicas.

DEATH-DEFYING DANGER

The 'Cage of Death' is an attraction that will either get you screaming with fear or squealing with delight. From the safety of a see-through container, you'll come face to face with Chopper, the second largest saltwater crocodile in captivity.

Chopper is a whopper!

SELFIE SPOT
Smile, crocodile! The 'Cage of Death' might not be the best place to take a selfie, but never mind: a photographer is on hand to 'snap' the moment.

CRUNCH, MUNCH

A special machine at the reptile park demonstrates the bite force of a crocodile. Watch the metal crocodile jaws make an easy meal of ice blocks, tiles or watermelons.

Museum & Art Gallery of the Northern Territory (MAGNT)

Father Ted Collins recorded the sounds of Cyclone Tracy when it hit Darwin early on Christmas morning in 1974. Today, the sounds of his audiotape fill the darkened sound booth at this museum. For locals who experienced Cyclone Tracy firsthand, the sounds of strong wind, breaking glass and crashing debris are things they'll never forget; some people still find the recordings too traumatic to listen to. For visitors, the sounds give an idea of what experiencing a cyclone that destroyed 70 per cent of Darwin's homes must have been like.

COLLECTION CATASTROPHE

When Cyclone Tracy hit in 1974, the Museum & Art Gallery of the Northern Territory was housed in Darwin's old Town Hall. The building and most of its collections were destroyed or damaged.

CELEBRITY CRITTER

A famous member of the museum is Sweetheart, a male crocodile that had a liking for attacking boats. In 1979, the croc was caught alive in Sweet's Lookout billabong, but sadly drowned soon after capture.

WEIRD WILDLIFE

In 2015, a special object became part of MAGNT's collection. Biologists at the museum identified what was initially thought to be a severed finger to be a sea squirt (a marine invertebrate animal) with a finger-like appearance!

EXPLORE MORE

DARWIN

Aquascene

At Doctors Gully in Darwin, the local wild fish are on to a good thing. Each day at high tide, visitors come armed with bread to handfeed hundreds of fish in the shallows. You might think that fish and fingers might not go well together, but at this marine sanctuary, the fish are harmless because they don't have dangerous barbs or teeth.

Tasty!

SNACK SPOT
Australian diver Carl Atkinson started the fish-feeding tradition in the 1950s. His original aim was to get some fish for dinner. However, the fish soon became his regular-visiting friends!

Australian Aviation Heritage Centre

On display at this museum are aeroplanes that have stories to tell about Darwin's long aviation history (did you know the city was subjected to 64 air raids during World War II?). There's a helicopter that helped with the Cyclone Tracy clean-up. There's a B-25 bomber whose crew, on its last flight, got lost over the desert because its compass was broken (they eventually returned to safety). There's even a fighter jet that crashed into mudflats near a Darwin suburb in 1985. Luckily that was another happy ending: the pilot survived, and the jet was restored.

Darwin danger plane

The tiger moth at the museum first took to the air at the start of World War II in 1939. These planes were designed so that fighter pilots could open their parachute as they jumped from the cockpit in an emergency.

Arghhhhhh!

Territory Wildlife Park

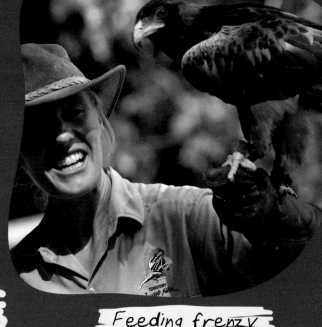

Darwin is part of the 'Top End', which is the most northern part of the Northern Territory. At the aquarium of the Territory Wildlife Park, in Berry Springs just south of Darwin, you can view the animals of a Top End river, a coastal mangrove community and a coral reef. There are other wildlife attractions too, such as a walk-through aviary and a nocturnal house. The latter turns a night animal's world upside-down. For the benefit of visitors, night becomes day, and day becomes night, so you can watch native woodland creatures go about their 'night' activities during the day. Is that as clear as day?

Goose on the loose

Calling all bird lovers! At Goose Lagoon, you can spy on birds such as magpie geese, egrets and herons from the privacy of a bird hide. Bring your binoculars!

Feeding frenzy

Every second day, a diver handfeeds the large female barramundi that live in the aquarium. It causes quite a commotion as the fish suck in their food with explosive speed!

I'm starting a new fashion trend!

WEIRD WILDLIFE

Everyone knows Nemo the famous clownfish is orange and white, right? Well, a Darwin ocellaris clownfish is a black-and-white version of Nemo and is unique to Darwin.

EXPLORE MORE
ULURU-KATA TJUTA NATIONAL PARK

KATA TJUTA

Kata Tjuta is located west of Uluru in the Central Australian desert. It has 36 ancient, giant rock domes, with the highest towering 546 metres above the ground (that's really tall, like four times the height of the Sydney Harbour Bridge). It's not surprising that its Aboriginal name, 'Kata Tjuta', means 'many heads'. In 1872, the rocks were named Mount Olga by English explorer Ernest Giles, in honour of Queen Olga of Württemberg (previously a state in Germany), but its Aboriginal name was reinstated in 1977.

WINDY WALK

The Valley of the Winds walk here has a bigger problem than wind. If temperatures reach 36°C, part of the track is closed.

ANIMAL COUNT

Reptiles and birds rule in the park. There are 73 reptile species and 178 kinds of birds, whereas only 21 mammals and four frog species.

SELFIE SPOT
Take a photo of you and your giant friends. Selfies rock! (Geddit?)

ULURU

Emu's rock too!

Uluru is a rock star (if you'll pardon the pun). Towering 348 metres above the ground, it is higher than the Eureka Tower in Melbourne (see p. 40). What's even more impressive is that some of this giant rock slab remains hidden underground. It is thought that it may extend up to 6 kilometres under the surface! Like all good rock stars, Uluru takes part in a dazzling light show. At sunrise and sunset, it appears to change colour.

ROOM TO ROAM

WATER

Uluru is not only high, it's also wide. If you walk around its base, you will roam for 9.4 kilometres. Don't forget your water bottle!

RUSTY RED

Oxidation of iron in the rock causes rust and gives Uluru its rusty red appearance.

ROCK CLIMBING

The traditional owners of Uluru ask that people do not climb the sacred rock, however, the climb is not prohibited. Sadly, more than 30 people have died attempting to reach the summit.

ROCK ART

There are wonderful examples of Aboriginal rock art around Uluru. People can easily damage the rock art, but water, dust, lichen, wasps and even swallows building nests can also harm it.

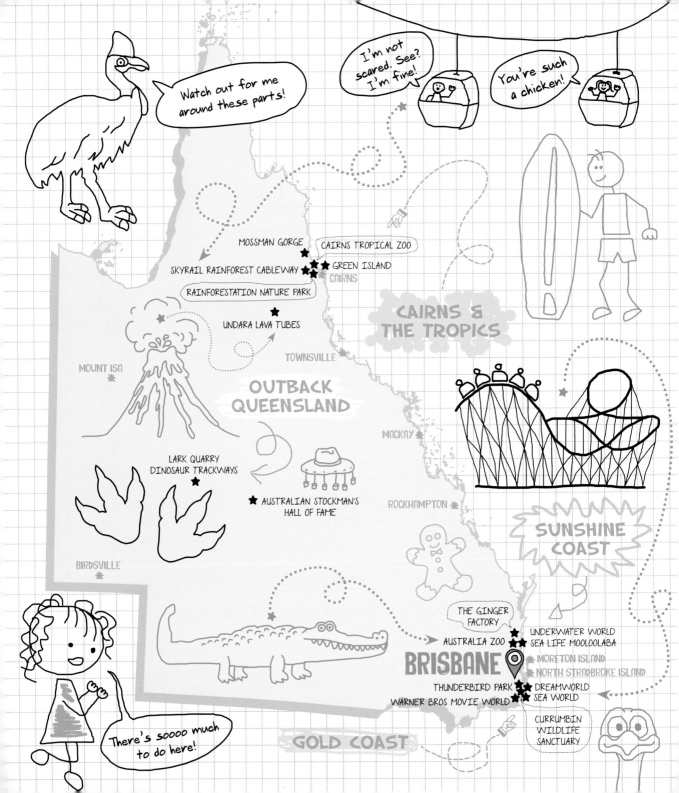

Bring on the sun!

QUEENSLAND

First penal colony

Moreton Bay Settlement opened in 1824 and was Brisbane's first penal colony. Its first residents were 30 convicts who were hardened criminals.

Oldest windmill

Convicts built Windmill Tower in Brisbane in the late 1820s. It is Australia's oldest surviving windmill.

Most remote town

Birdsville is Australia's most isolated outback town. It is located on the edge of the Simpson Desert. The local policeman patrols an area about the size of the United Kingdom!

BRISBANE is the capital city of Queensland and Australia's third largest city by population. In 1824, Brisbane became a convict settlement. The first site chosen for the settlement was an area called Humpybong, which is an Aboriginal word that means 'dead house', although HUMPYBONG was very much alive with mosquitoes! By 1842, the convict settlement closed and soon the 'River City', as Brisbane became known, welcomed free settlers.

Sunniest island

You'll be drawn to this island! Magnetic Island is thought to be the sunniest island on Australia's northern coast. Each year, it has more than 300 days of sunshine.

FUN FACTS

Oldest house

The oldest surviving home in Brisbane is Newstead House. It was built in 1846. Initially, it was a small Georgian cottage, but after renovations in 1867 it turned into the mansion it is today.

Most big things

How big am I?

Australia is famous for its BIG roadside attractions, such as the Big Pineapple, the Big Mud Crab and the Big Ned Kelly. Queensland has the most big things out of all the states in Australia. Which one are you a BIG fan of?

Wettest place

Tully holds the Australian record for the highest annual rainfall in a populated area. In 1950, it received a sopping 7.93 metres of rain. The town has a giant Golden Gumboot as a monument to the rains – but perhaps a giant Wet Welly would be more appropriate!

Most creepy exhibit

Brisbane's Commissariat Store Museum has a very creepy exhibit. It's a jar full of fingertips! Convicts used to cut off the tips of their fingers in order to get out of doing hard labour!

That's a tad extreme.

TOP SPOTS

BRISBANE

Brisbane Botanic Gardens Mt Coot-tha

There's nothing like a game of hide-and-seek to explore a shady exotic rainforest. The Hide 'n' Seek Children's Trail at these botanic gardens is interactive, informative and, most importantly, buckets of fun. Did you know that Mt Coot-tha used to be called Kuta, an Aboriginal word that means 'place of honey'? Grab a trail map, read the clues and hunt for the botanical treasures.

HERBARIUM HISTORY

The Herbarium houses more than 830,000 specimens. Some of these are older than the gardens themselves, such as the specimens Joseph Banks collected on his 1770 journey with Captain James Cook.

FLOOD & MUD

Between 1870 and 1974, the botanic gardens have had to withstand eight major floods. Sure, trees need water to survive, but that's taking things a bit far!

WEIRD WILDLIFE

This area is home to small black native Australian bees called sugarbag bees or sweet bees. You don't need to run for cover though – these bees are stingless!

Lone Pine Koala Sanctuary

Koalas Jack and Jill were the stars of the Lone Pine Koala Sanctuary in 1927 (this wildlife park had only two koalas back then). By the 1930s, koalas were not the only attraction. A German shepherd with a koala or two riding on its back like a jockey used to greet the visitors. Then, a snake got in on the act and draped itself around the dog too! Today, at the world's first (and largest) koala sanctuary, you can hold a koala, an eagle, an owl or a snake. You can also feed kangaroos.

Gosh, I'm sooo tired.

SPECIAL KOALA

In the 1970s, visitors to the sanctuary got to see an unusual koala named Kalbar. It had white fur! Albino koalas are extremely rare.

OLD AGE

Lone Pine holds the world record for having had the oldest koala in captivity. Sarah the koala died in 2001 at the record-breaking age of 23!

WHAT'S IN A NAME?
In 1865, Lone Pine was a cotton farm. The owners planted a single hoop pine tree. Today, this very old pine tree is by the entrance building.

MUNCH-TIME!

In 1988, the sanctuary established its own eucalyptus plantation in order to provide food for all the koalas. That was smart thinking, because there are about 130 koalas at the sanctuary today.

Did someone say 'munch-time'?

Queensland Museum

Like all good museums, the Queensland Museum has been an avid collector, particularly when it comes to anything to do with the cultural and natural heritage of Queensland and its neighbouring areas. Back in 1862, when it first opened and was known as the Queensland Philosophical Society, the museum displayed its then smallish collection in a windmill on Wickham Tce. These days, it has millions of specimens and artefacts displayed in four different museum locations.

Ewww, creeepy crawlies!

TOP THREE

Dinosaurs are a real hit at the museum. The three most visited are *Tyrannosaurus rex*, *Triceratops* and *Muttaburrasaurus langdoni*.

BIG BUG

The museum has many live (and not so live) specimens on display. Northern Queensland's own giant burrowing cockroach is a show stopper. It's the world's heaviest cockroach, weighing up to 30 grams. Wouldn't want to encounter one of those in your backyard!

Those cockroaches look tasty!

WAGON WONDERLAND

The Cobb+Co. Museum is part of the Queensland Museum. The Cobb+Co. company operated a horse-drawn coach service in Queensland from 1866. The drivers used to ride in America's Wild West – that's cowboy country!

WEIRD WILDLIFE
The muttaburrasaurus roamed in Australia about 100 million years ago. A partial skeleton of this dinosaur was first discovered in Qld.

Sir Thomas Brisbane Planetarium

It's fitting that the planetarium at Mt Coot-tha is named after a space enthusiast. Sir Thomas Brisbane was the governor of NSW between 1821 and 1825; during his time as governor, he undertook a survey of the southern skies. Today, stargazing guests can watch space shows in the Cosmic Skydome at the planetarium. With show names like Cosmic Collisions, you're sure to be on the edge of your seat — and the universe!

Hey, I want to get in on the fun too! I'll be good. I promise.

SELFIE SPOT
Snap a selfie of you and the sculpture of Konstantin Tsiolkovsky. What's the Russian rocket scientist looking up at?

Streets Beach

This attraction's name is a clue to its location. The beach is at South Bank, in the middle of the city. How can that be? It's easy. This riverside swimming beach, with its lagoon, white sand and palm trees, is artificial. It's a beach without the danger of pounding waves, dangerous rips and great white sharks!

SWIMMING SAFETY

The beach has the benefits of many other swimming beaches. There are lifeguards on duty seven days a week.

EXPLORE MORE

BRISBANE

Moreton Island

Is this an island with a spelling mistake? Well, Captain James Cook named the island's headland Cape Morton in 1770, and then in 1799, explorer Matthew Flinders gave the island the name Moreton Island (along with one extra letter)! Moreton Island is the world's third largest sand island and is known as 'the Gem of South-East Queensland' — that's 'gem' with a 'g' not a 'j', Matthew Flinders!

The sand surf is up!

Sand adventures

Where there is a sand island, there are often sand dunes. Little Sand Hills and Big Sand Hills on the island are ideal places for sand boarding (standing up) and sand tobogganing (sitting or lying down).

Island lighting

In 1857, the Cape Moreton Lighthouse shone its light for the first time to aid passing ships. Convicts helped construct the lighthouse, which was the first to be built in Queensland.

ACTION & ADVENTURE

Snorkelling in a shipwreck sounds like fun, but what about 15 shipwrecks? Tangalooma Wrecks is a site just off Moreton Island where 15 ships were sunk on purpose to act as a breakwater for small boats. It's a diving and snorkelling mecca!

North Stradbroke Island

Off the coast of Brisbane in Moreton Bay lies North Stradbroke Island, the world's second largest sand island (they love their sand islands up this way! *See* p. 106). Known to many of the locals as 'Straddie', this island is bustling with wildlife. The traditional island owners, the Quandamooka people, definitely know it bustles with wildlife because they call the island Minjerribah, which means 'place of many mosquitoes'!

Floating food

In 1942 during World War II, debris from an American ship heading to Brisbane washed up on North Stradbroke Island. The islanders were treated to tins of coffee, bags of cotton sheets and turkeys, which were destined for Thanksgiving plates!

Sun, surf & sand

The list of adventures you can have on North Stradbroke Island often start with the letter 's' … you can surf, swim, sea kayak, snorkel and sand board!

Sssounds sssuper!

WHAT'S IN A NAME?
About half of the island is a protected national park called Naree Budjong Djara, which means 'My Mother Earth' to the island's traditional owners.

Island isolation

In 1891, a person with leprosy was sent to Dunwich on North Stradbroke Island's west coast and put in isolation in a tent. In all, about 80 leprosy patients were isolated at Dunwich up until 1907.

Queensland Maritime Museum

When you think of boats and the ocean, what colour springs to mind? Blue, foamy white, sea-green or aquamarine? How about bright pink? That's the colour of Jessica Watson's yacht called *Ella's Pink Lady*. This Queensland sailor made the headlines in 2010 when she became the youngest person to sail solo, nonstop and unassisted, around the world. She was 16 years old. Today, her pink yacht lives at the Queensland Maritime Museum along with other boats that have their own stories to share.

SELFIE SPOT
Go aboard HMAS *Diamantina* and take your pick of where to take a selfie – in the engine room, in the captain's quarters or inside the medical bay.

I want to sail around the world too!

Cool pool
The dry dock at the museum has had an interesting past. In 1899, the Queensland Amateur Swimming Association used it as a swimming pool!

Watery woes
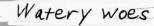

In January 2011, floods hit Queensland. Despite being designed for water, some of the boats at the museum suffered flood damage. HMAS *Diamantina* floated off her blocks in the dry dock and suffered two leaks, while CLS 2 *Carpentaria* rolled on her side.

Story Bridge

What's the story with Story Bridge? Firstly, its consulting engineer was J.J.C. Bradfield who oversaw the building of the Sydney Harbour Bridge. Secondly, it was built in the 1930s to provide relief work during the Great Depression. Thirdly, it hasn't always been called Story Bridge (before it opened, it was known as Jubilee Bridge). Fourthly, you can climb it or abseil from it!

Down, down, down

What goes up, must come down. For the abseil, you descend 30 metres down the anchor pier. (Sorry if you're under ten, but you have to be ten or older to participate.)

The Workshops Rail Museum

If you like trains, head to this rail museum in North Ipswich, just west of Brisbane. You'll be excused if you don't know where to race to first though. You could drive a train in the diesel train simulator, climb aboard a guard's van, look for a cowcatcher on the object wall or see the largest model railway in Queensland!

TOOT TOOT TOOOOOOT

Oi! Moooove it!

NASTY PAST-Y
A cowcatcher was a device at the front of a train that cleared objects, such as cows, off the tracks!

EXPLORE MORE
CAIRNS & THE TROPICS

CAIRNS TROPICAL ZOO

This is not the place where you'll find a polar bear. Cairns is in the far north of tropical Queensland, so the zoo residents reside in warm and wet conditions. One experience on offer at the zoo is to have breakfast with a koala. You don't have to worry about the koala munching on the fresh fruit, cereals or waffles though. Luckily for you, they eat mainly eucalyptus leaves.

Stay on your toes!

WEIRD WILDLIFE
Southern cassowaries live in the tropical rainforests of north-east Queensland. With dagger-like claws that can slice through predators, these animals are considered the world's most dangerous bird. Best to encounter them in the safe confines of Cairns Tropical Zoo then!

GREEN ISLAND

Green Island is a small island just 27 kilometres north-east of Cairns. It's part of the Great Barrier Reef, which has about 1050 islands and cays. Green Island is one of a kind: it's the only coral cay out of the 300 on the Great Barrier Reef that has a rainforest on it! Take a ride in a glass-bottom boat and spy on the residents lurking below in Green Island's surrounding waters.

ISLAND SURVIVAL

In 1889, coconut trees were planted on Green Island to provide shipwrecked sailors with a good supply of food, liquid and shelter.

MOSSMAN GORGE

Mossman Gorge, located in the Daintree Rainforest, is the place for budding biologists. The area has one of the wettest climates in Australia, which is good news for all the plants and animals that live in the ancient rainforest. How about playing a game of I-spy (with my little eye)? Look for an animal or a plant from Queensland beginning with b ... Boyd's forest dragon, back scratcher ginger ...

ROOM TO ROAM
The Daintree Rainforest is the last remnant of the oldest surviving rainforest in the world. It covers 120,000 hectares.

I hide out here too!

RAINFORESTATION NATURE PARK

What do you get when you cross a boat with a truck? An Army Duck (or DUKW), of course! These World War II amphibious vehicles, with their six wheels, rudders and propellers, let visitors to Rainforestation Nature Park ride over ancient tropical rainforest as well as splash across a murky brown river. At this park, near Kuranda, you can also throw a boomerang, play a didgeridoo and watch spear throwing.

SKYRAIL RAINFOREST CABLEWAY

Skyrail's cable cars travel just metres above the spectacular tropical rainforests of north Queensland, as well as through the canopy, for a distance of 7.5 kilometres — and they do so rain or shine. After all, rainforests are all about rain. A tropical rainforest wouldn't be one officially if it didn't get at least 1.3 metres of rain each year!

Whoa, it's so high!

But what a view!

EXPLORE MORE
GOLD COAST

HEY! Get off my property!

CURRUMBIN WILDLIFE SANCTUARY

It only takes one person to make a difference, and that's how this sanctuary came about. Alex Griffiths was a flower grower in the 1940s. When wild lorikeets started eating his flowers, Alex started to feed the birds instead. Soon, he and the lorikeets became a tourist attraction. Then, by 1947, the sanctuary opened. Today, visitors can carry on Alex's tradition and feed the lorikeets too. Watch out though: the birds like to land on your arms and head!

ROOM TO ROAM
If you see an emu wandering about the 27-hectare sanctuary, don't worry: it hasn't escaped. The emus are free to roam most of the land.

DREAMWORLD

Dreamworld has rides that are a thrill a minute. With scream machines such as Tower of Terror II, Pandamonium and Tail Spin, you are sure to scream yourself silly. Dreamworld also features some of the movie star heroes from Dreamworks, such as Shrek and Kung Fu Panda. In fact, Kung Fu Panda land is called Land of Awesomeness, which pretty much sums up the whole of Dreamworld!

So exciting!

STARS & STRIPES
One wild attraction at Dreamworld is Tiger Island, where you get to watch Bengal and Sumatran tigers leap, jump and climb trees.

SEA WORLD

This marine animal park can be summed up in one word — splashtacular! Sea World has shows in which dolphins and sea lions splash their way into people's hearts. There are also jetski riders performing heart-stopping stunts. But perhaps the most splashtacular of all is the chance to spray your family and friends from one of the boats in Castaway Bay, an interactive adventure playground. On the Battle Boats attraction, there are more than 55 water cannons, so take aim and fire!

Splashtacular!

THUNDERBIRD PARK

Queensland has the world's largest thunder-egg mine. Formed in prehistoric volcanic lava, thunder eggs are fossils that are about 200 million years old. At Thunderbird Park, you can have a go at thunder-egg fossicking. The real fun begins when the thunder eggs are cut open to reveal the beautiful patterns and colours inside.

WARNER BROS. MOVIE WORLD

The thrill-o-meter is always on maximum at Movie World, where movie-themed rides provide the extreme, while you provide the scream. Try thrilling rides like Batwing Spaceshot or Superman Escape. You can also watch a Hollywood blockbuster stunt show. Action ... rolling!

SELFIE SPOT
You'll have the chance to ask 'what's up, doc?' when you take a selfie with Bugs Bunny or one of his Looney Tunes friends.

EXPLORE MORE
SUNSHINE COAST

AUSTRALIA ZOO

The Irwin family, a bunch of true-blue wildlife warriors, started Australia Zoo back in 1970, except back then the zoo was called Beerwah Reptile and Fauna Park. Steve Irwin, aka the Crocodile Hunter, grew up with wildlife-loving parents and a house brimming with injured and rescued animals. It's not surprising then that Steve caught his first venomous snake at age six and captured his first croc at nine! Tragically, Steve died in 2006, but his beloved Australia Zoo carries on his important work of wildlife conservation.

ANIMAL ACTION

Australia Zoo's Crocoseum was inspired by the movie *Gladiator*. The specially designed arena is where visitors get to see crocodiles, huge snakes, elephants and birds. It's also the place where the audience can scream out Steve Irwin's famous saying, 'Crikey!'.

CARING FOR ANIMALS

Australia Zoo Wildlife Hospital is dedicated to Steve's mother who died in 2000. When Steve was a boy, he and his mother would often stop on the side of the road on the way to school to rescue the joeys from dead kangaroos!

PAT A DRAGON

Australia Zoo has a unique animal encounter. It's with a komodo dragon, which is a giant lizard — not an actual dragon! You're allowed to touch its back, but not its face, head or any other part of its body.

WEIRD WILDLIFE
The echidna has no teeth. It uses its long, sticky tongue to eat ants, termites and earthworms. At Australia Zoo, you can have an echidna lick food off your toes!

That guy looks like me!

THE GINGER FACTORY

Is this a ginger factory or a themed tourist park? It's both! At the Ginger Factory in Yandina, you can watch ginger products being whipped up in the ginger factory, decorate your own gingerbread man biscuit and hunt for the Gingerbread Man on the Overboard Boat Ride. And if you run, run as fast as you can, you can jump on the 100-year-old cane train and take a ride through the tropical gardens.

I'm seriously tasty!

SELFIE SPOT
Fancy a selfie with the Gingerbread Man? Then this is the perfect place!

UNDERWATER WORLD SEA LIFE MOOLOOLABA

Imagine swimming with sharks, without the safety of a cage. At this aquarium, you can dive or snorkel with sharks, stingrays and fish — if you dare! You can also go behind the scenes to be a seal trainer for a day and learn about the tricks that the seals perform at the shows. Here's a tip: if you put one hand on a seal's side and flick up the thumb of your other hand, the seal will start making barking noises! The other attractions at Underwater World, such as Otter Creek and Seahorse Sanctuary, also get the thumbs up!

BLUE, WHITE OR BROWN?

If you want to see the largest collection of jellyfish in Australia, then head to Jellyfish Kingdom at Underwater World. Blue blubber jellyfish are on display here. The strange thing is that in southern Queensland, these jellyfish are indeed blue, whereas in Sydney, they're white or brown.

Yeah? Lets see what you got.

I LOVE doing tricks!

EXPLORE MORE
OUTBACK QUEENSLAND

AUSTRALIAN STOCKMAN'S HALL OF FAME

Hats off to the stock workers, pioneers and unsung heroes of remote Australia. It's no surprise that this outback heritage attraction is situated in Longreach, at the junction of a number of stock routes. It also makes sense that the centre's design is inspired by outback farm buildings, silos and water tanks. The Outback Stockman's Show features trick horses and dogs and a singing, guitar-playing stockman on a bull!

WHAT'S IN A NAME?
Qantas and the Ford Motor Company have each named vehicles after Longreach.

DRINK STOP
Teamsters, or bullockers, used to stop at Longreach, which had a large waterhole for their stock animals to have a drink.

OUTBACK DISPLAY
The centre considers itself the custodian of the bush. It has five themed galleries and more than 1200 items on display.

LARK QUARRY DINOSAUR TRACKWAYS

In the movie *Jurassic Park*, there was a scary scene in which dinosaurs stampeded. The inspiration for this came all the way from Lark Quarry Dinosaur Trackways, which has the **ONLY RECORDED EVIDENCE OF A DINOSAUR STAMPEDE ON EARTH**. There are more than 3300 dinosaur tracks at this site, which is near Winton. The stampede took place about 95 million years ago when a large meat-eating dinosaur chased smaller two-legged dinosaurs, many as tiny as chickens!

NASTY PAST-Y
The footprints of the attacking dinosaur appear to match the footprint of Banjo, a dinosaur discovered near Winton in 2006.

UNDARA LAVA TUBES

Flowing molten lava produced the lava tubes in this area about 190,000 years ago. The tubes are like hidden pipelines under the ground. Undara is an Aboriginal word that means 'long way', which is the perfect name because Undara Volcanic National Park is home to one of the world's longest lava tube cave systems.

RAIN, RAIN
If there is plenty of rain, the tubes fill with water. Instead of walking through the tubes, you get to swim your way along them, so remember to pack your swimsuit!

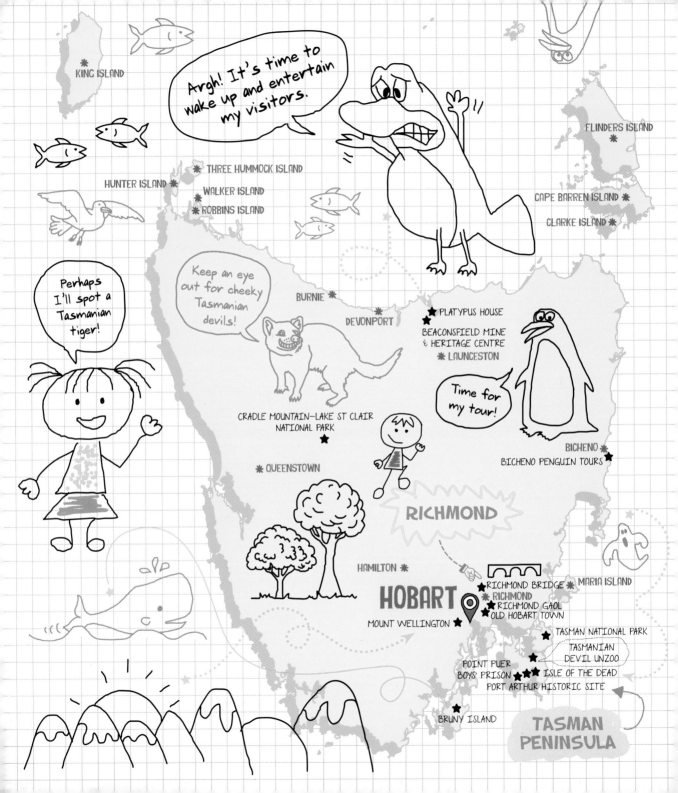

ACE!

TASMANIA

First name

Hobart was first called Hobart Town, but in 1881 the word 'town' was dropped from its name, because by then its population had grown and it was a city!

HOBART is the second oldest city in Australia and the capital of Tasmania, the island state of the country. In 1642, the Dutch navigator Abel Tasman called the island Van Diemen's Land. This name would come to be associated with convicts, who were sent to the island from 1803. However, convicts were not the only residents with rough, tough reputations. Antarctic whalers also called Van Diemen's Land home in the 1800s. It's surprising that these residents were not at times very lovable, because Tasmania might perhaps be one of the most lovable places in Australia. After all, it is shaped like a heart!

Oldest theatre

Hobart's Theatre Royal, which opened in 1837, is the oldest working theatre in Australia. In the early days, dubious characters used to visit the theatre to watch entertainment such as cockfights!

Tallest tree

At just over 100 metres tall, the Arve Valley's giant swamp gum named 'Centurion' is not only the world's tallest eucalypt, but also the tallest hardwood tree and tallest flowering plant.

FUN FACTS

Oldest sailor

Hobart is famous for the Sydney Hobart Yacht Race. The oldest sailor ever to take part in the race was 86-year-old John Walker. The year was 2008. He had already taken part in the race 24 times!

Funniest place names

Tasmania has its fair share of funny place names, such as CAPE GRIM and EGGS AND BACON BAY. Sometimes it has to share its names with other states. Nowhere Else is not only in Tasmania, but in South Australia too! So clearly Nowhere Else is somewhere else …

First apples

Tasmania grows most of its apples south of Hobart. The early settlers grew apples on the island too. From the 1820s, apples were transported to other parts of Australia, earning Tasmania the nickname the 'Apple Isle'.

Tasmania is the apple of my eye!

TOP SPOTS

HOBART

Battery Point Sculpture Trail

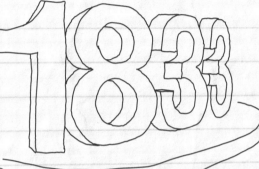

If you see the big numbers 1833, you'll know that you have stumbled across the Battery Point Sculpture Trail. There are nine numerical sculptures along this walking trail, and each one relates to the history and heritage of Battery Point. The 313 sculpture floating in the Derwent River represents the 313 vessels launched from the Battery Point slipyards in the 1800s. Can you find out which famous Tasmanian actor is the inspiration for the 1909 sculpture?

BLAST FROM THE PAST

Battery Point is named after the battery of guns that were erected in 1818 to protect Hobart Town from enemies. Luckily, the guns were never fired.

Cascades Female Factory Historic Site

Sounding more like a factory that churns out women, the Cascades Female Factory was Tasmania's main women's prison between 1828 and 1856. The purpose of the institution was to house and reform female convicts. To help pay for costs, the convicts undertook needlework and laundry work. Life was harsh at the factory, and what's worse was that many female inmates raised their children there. It's now a place where you can be transported back to convict times with displays and dramatised theatre performances.

NASTY PAST-Y
Punishment for the women included shaving or cutting off their hair, or being forced to wear heavy iron collars!

Mawson's Huts Replica Museum

Sir Douglas Mawson was a scientist, a polar explorer and an overall hero who led the Australasian Antarctic Expedition of 1911—14, which departed from Hobart. The real Mawson huts are still in Antarctica, however, full-scale replicas of the huts were built in Hobart in 2013. The items on display in the replica huts give you an idea of what expedition life would have been like in Mawson's day. The huts come complete with replica graffiti on the walls and some very real-looking (but stuffed) huskies.

ANTARCTIC TERRITORY
AUSTRALIAN
1911 MAWSON
5D

NASTY PAST-Y
Many items have been donated to the museum, including an original sledge used by Mawson. Amazingly, it was found on a rubbish dump. Bet it smelt nasty!

Mount Wellington

Give three cheers to the Great Depression workers of the 1930s. Thanks to them, a road winds its way to the summit of Mt Wellington. Unless you travel there by car or bus, you would definitely be crying out 'Are we there yet?' because Mt Wellington is 1271 metres high — that's a long way up!

(ROCKY PIPES)

The Organ Pipes on Mt Wellington are really old – like dinosaur old. Formed during the Jurassic period, these vertical rock formations are popular with rock climbers, particularly very daring ones.

I'm nearly there!

EXPLORE MORE
RICHMOND

OLD HOBART TOWN

You'll feel like a giant walking around this model village, which is a 'mini me' of Hobart Town as it was in the 1820s. There are 500 people dotted about the town, although they are all miniature figurines made from clay. The village's 60 buildings are based on historical records and plans. Even the trees in the model village are mini-sized, despite being more than 20 years old!

FAMOUS FOUR

A hand-drawn map helps you find your way around the village. The map challenges you to find four special figurines: a woman hitting a snake with a stick, a boy falling out of a tree, a Tasmanian tiger and a man skinning a kangaroo!

STILL STANDING

Ten out of the 60 buildings in the model village can still be found in Hobart today. Can you figure out which ones they are?

SELFIE SPOT
Take a selfie with a convict chain gang or with a man who has stepped in a slop bucket!

RICHMOND BRIDGE

Convicts knew all about hard labour. When they built Richmond Bridge, they had to cut sandstone from a quarry at nearby Butcher's Hill and transport it in hand carts to the building site. For about 17 long months, the convicts slavishly built the six-arch bridge over Coal River. Although it's needed many repairs over the years — the first took place only a year after the bridge opened! — the convicts must be commended for a job well done because Richmond Bridge is Australia's oldest surviving bridge.

How clever!

BUILT TO LAST

With about 200,000 people visiting the bridge each year, it is just as well the convicts did such a fine job!

RICHMOND GAOL

The year 1825 was a busy year for convicts in Richmond. This is when they built the oldest part of Richmond Gaol, but the jail ended up being a bit of a work-in-progress project, with the last of it being finished in 1840. Today, Richmond Gaol is Australia's oldest intact jail. The flogging yard gives a glimpse into the brutal life convicts endured. For example, in 1834, 142 men received a total of 4425 lashes. What's worse, the people dishing out the floggings were usually convicts or ex-convicts themselves!

NASTY PAST-Y

Between 1842 and 1845, Solomon Bleay, the colony hangman, was also a prisoner at Richmond Gaol. That didn't stop him doing his job though. He was simply escorted to the hangings and back to his cell!

EXPLORE MORE
TASMAN PENINSULA

ISLE OF THE DEAD

As its name suggests, this island was for the dead! The small island is situated in the harbour off Port Arthur and about 1000 burials took place there between 1833 and 1877. This graveyard for the Port Arthur penal settlement did not only contain convicts. It was also the final resting place for soldiers, civilians and their families. Don't expect to find 1000 headstones in the cemetery though, because convicts were generally not allowed to have their graves marked.

HIGH & MIGHTY

Free settlers were usually buried on higher ground at the north end of the island, away from the convicts!

POINT PUER BOYS' PRISON

Near the Isle of the Dead is Point Puer, which was home to a British Empire 'first' — this was the site of the first reformatory designed especially for young male convicts. The 3000 boys who were imprisoned at Point Puer between 1834 and 1849 wouldn't have been overjoyed that they were making history though. The first 60 boy prisoners, who arrived in December 1833, would certainly not have been thrilled, because they were given the task of building the prison!

NASTY PAST-Y
Punishment was harsh at the boys' prison. One poor lad was put in solitary confinement for three whole days just for throwing bread at another boy!

PORT ARTHUR HISTORIC SITE

This was not a place for a faint-hearted convict. George Arthur, the Lieutenant-Governor of Van Diemen's Land, wanted this particular penal settlement to be 'a place of terror'. Escape would have been on the minds of the convicts, but the steep sea cliffs acted like prison bars, and the armed soldiers and dogs also acted as deterrents. Escapes and attempted escapes were still made though. One bizarre attempt was by Billy Hunt, who disguised himself as a kangaroo. Unfortunately for Billy, a soldier thought he was a real kangaroo and tried to shoot him!

Oogedy boogedy!

BOO!
The Port Arthur Ghost Tour might get your teeth chattering as you explore darkened ruins and historic buildings while listening to tales of paranormal sightings — otherwise known as ghosts!

TASMANIAN DEVIL UNZOO

Do I have any holes in my teeth?

Tasmanian devils are the stars of this conservation centre at Taranna, recently renamed 'Unzoo' because all the fences have been taken down so the animals are free to roam! From the safety of a viewing dome, you can get up close and personal with these fierce and feisty carnivorous marsupials. Watch as they scream, snarl and screech over meat and crunch through bones. These little devils also share the limelight with other Australian native animals at the centre.

WHAT'S IN A NAME?
Early settlers called them 'devils' because of the animals' loud shrieks (which sound like the devil) and their red ears (which look like the devil)!

EXPLORE MORE
TASMANIA

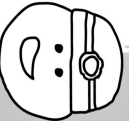

I hope I find some gold!

BEACONSFIELD MINE & HERITAGE CENTRE

On 25 April 2006, Beaconsfield hit the headlines when an earthquake triggered a rockfall in a gold mine. The remarkable story of two miners who survived for 14 days trapped 950 metres below the surface was soon broadcast around the world. Today, a display at the centre retells this incredible tale. There are also old mining relics, such as a water wheel, as well as a 3D holographic display that reveals the underground workings of a gold mine.

HANDS-ON HELP

There are many hands-on displays at the mine. In fact, here's a handy hint: if you see a yellow symbol of a hand, you'll know the display is interactive!

BICHENO PENGUIN TOURS

Cat and dog attacks once made the penguin population at Bicheno plummet to just 40 birds. Luckily, the penguins at the rookery are now thriving. Watch the penguins waddle along their sandy 'highways' as they make their nightly journey from the sea to their burrows. It pays to wear covered shoes because the **PENGUINS HAVE BEEN KNOWN TO BITE TOES!**

Argghh! Keep those bright lights away from me!

SELFIE SPOT
This is not the place for selfies or cameras. Camera flashes scare off the penguins.

My eyes are frazzled!

BRUNY ISLAND

Bruny Island is not a puny island. At about 100 kilometres long, it consists of two land masses that are joined by a long, narrow strip of land known as 'the Neck'. There's no public transport on the island, so it's helpful to bring a car with you. Luckily, a ferry service to the island lets you (well, your parents) take a car onboard!

NIGHT LIGHT

If you want to watch Tasmanian mutton-birds and little penguins return to Bruny Island at dusk, place red cellophane over your torch, remembering never to point the torch at the water or the birds.

I'm back!

WHALE OF A TIME

If you visit Bruny Island between May and July, or September and December, keep your eyes peeled for a very large attraction – migrating humpback and southern right whales. You won't miss them: they're huge!

PLATYPUS HOUSE

Welcome to monotreme territory. (A monotreme is a mammal that lays eggs.) Platypus House, located near Beaconsfield, isn't just home to one type of monotreme — the platypus. It also has the only other kind of monotreme — the echidna. Taking flash photos of the platypuses is not frowned upon here because these odd-looking creatures swim and dive underwater with their nose, ears and eyes firmly shut!

WEIRD WILDLIFE

Echidnas aren't being bad mannered when they snort and blow their noses. You try removing dirt from your nasal cavities without being able to use a handkerchief!

Do you have to snort?

Index

Index

Index

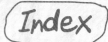

Index

About the author

Janine Scott has written many books for children. She caught the travel bug once again while she was writing *Explore Australia: the Kid Edition*, because this vast continent, nicknamed 'Down Under', is full of fascinating stories of colonies, convicts and courage. Janine likes to 'go off the beaten track' as she writes to discover all the cool stuff about a place. Did you know Sydney's first zoo was situated on Billy Goat Swamp, that 200 crocodiles have an inner-city Darwin address, and in 1835 Batman established Melbourne? Janine hopes that the travel tales and trivia in this book will open up the world of Australia for all young explorers.

Acknowledgements

The publisher would like to acknowledge the following individuals and organisations:

Illustrations
Penny Black Design; David Thompson; Julie Hally, adapted from illustrations by Igor Zakowski/SH, toallyjamie/SH, Christophe BOISSON/SH, larryrains/SH, Virinaflora/SH, lineartestpilot/SH, Irina N/SH, SvitlalskyBros/SH, Ohn Mar/SH, Patrick Rolands/SH, Seamartini Graphics/SH, jorgen mcleman/SH, yayasya/SH, vallustration/SH, Teguh Mujiono/SH, Robj/SH, novkota1/SH, demonique/SH, Matthew Cole/SH, Banzainer/SH, advent/SH, Yayayoyo/SH, eazu/SH, Sarawut Padungkwan/SH, Knumina Studios/SH, Jonanovic Dejan/SH, Seohwa Kim/SH

Photography credits (clockwise from top left)
Page x (a) R. Gino Santa Marie/SH, (b) Peter Waters/SH, (c) Joe Belanger/SH, (d) Katarina Christenson/SH, (e) Matt9122/SH, (f) Michal Ninger/SH; xi (a) Meister Photos/SH, (b) Salim October/SH, (c) Henner Damke/SH, (d) Pe3k/SH, (e) Chanwit Polpakdee/SH, (f) Lakeview Images/SH, (g) A Cotton Photo/SH, (h) Paul Looyen/SH; 4 David Steele/SH; 5 Visun Khanksem/SH; 6 (a) Thorsten Rust/SH, (b) TranceDrumer/SH; 7 bbofdon/SH; 8 siwamut/SH; 9 Aleksandar Todorovic/SH; 11 (a) Aleksandar Todorovic/SH, (b) 360b/SH; 12 James Horan/DNSW; 13 (a) Jordan Tan/SH, (b) bluehand/SH, (c) aaltair/SH; 14 col/SH; 15 (a) ben Bryant/SH, (b) FiledIMAGE/SH; 17 (a) col/SH, (b) ian woolcock/SH; 19 Pip Blackwood/DNSW; 21 (a)Hamilton Lund/DNSW, (b) Julia Zakharova/SH; 23 Mark Higgins/SH; 26 (a) Eddie Misic/VC, (b) VC; 27 Dan Breckoldt/SH; 28 (a) Phillip Minnis/SH, (b) National Museum of Australia/VC; 29 (a) Dan Breckwoldt/SH, (b) VC; 33 GeorgeMPhotography/SH; 34 VV; 35 VV; 36 Andrey Bayda/SH; 37 (a) matiascausa/SH, (b) Mark Higgins/SH; 39 (a) Piotr Krzselak/SH, (b) & (c) artshock/SH; 40 VV; 41 (a) Roberto Seba/VV, (b) & (c) Luke Hally; 42 (a) Relvin Gonzalez/SH, (b) Melbourne Star Observation Wheel/VV; 43 (a) VV, (b) Luke Hally; 44 (a) Boyloso/SH, (b) Luke Hally; 45 Julia Kuleshova/SH; 51 VV;

52 fon thachakul/SH; 53 VV; 58 Gary Unwin/SH; 59 (a) Ekaterina Kamenetsky/SH, (b) Timothy Craig Lubcke/SH; 61 SATC; 62 Timothy Craig Lubcke/SH; 63 (a) SATC, (b) Everett Historical; 65 InavanHateren/SH; 66 (a) Michael Leslie/SH; 67 Tim De Boek/SH; 68 K.A.Willis/SH; 69 John White Photos/SH; 74 imagevixen/SH; 75 (a) Felix Lipov/SH, (b) TWA; 76 Curioso/SH; 77 Andres Ello/SH; 78 (a) Marcella Miriello/SH, (b) Jordan Tan/SH; 79 (a) JLRPhotography/SH, (b) Ashley Whitworth/SH; 80 Gordon Bell/SH; 81 Alberto Loyo/SH; 82 TWA; 83 Aneta Waberska/SH; 84 kkaplin/SH; 85 Andrey Nosik/SH; 90 Susan Flashman/SH; 91 (a) TNT, (b) TNT; 92 holbox/SH; 93 (a) TNT, (b) TNT; 94 NatalieJean/SH; 95 TNT; 96 Noradoa/SH; 97 Stanislav Fosenbauer/SH; 102 (a) Paul Bardett/SH, (b) covenant/SH; 103 Covenant/SH; 104 Andrew Burgess/SH; 105 (a) Lakeview Images/SH, (b) ChameleonsEye/SH; 106 Pete Niesen/SH; 107 covenant/SH; 108 (a) ChameleonsEye/SH, (b) SF Photo/SH; 109 ChameleonsEye/SH; 110 John Carnemolla/SH; 11 Marco Saracco/SH; 112 Neale Cousland/SH; 113 (a) & (b) ChameleonsEye/SH; 114 Damian Herde/SH; 115 Julz/SH; 116 (a) Peter Lik/TEQ, (b) TEQ; 123 (a) Bockman 1973/SH, (b) ian woolcock/SH; 124 (a) & (b) Ekaterina Kamenetsky/SH; 125 (a) Ekaterina Kamenetsky/SH, (b) MelBrackstone/SH; 126 Full Bottle/SH; 127 (a) Jacqui Martin/SH, (b) Susan Flashman/SH; 128 ChameleonsEye/SH; Rob Bayer/SH

ABBREVIATIONS
DNSW – Destination New South Wales
SATC – South Australian Tourism Commission
SH – Shutterstock.com
TEQ – Tourism and Events Queensland
TNT – Tourism Northern Territory
TWA – Tourism Western Australia
VC – Visit Canberra
VV – Visions of Victoria

Acknowledgements cont.

The publisher would like to acknowledge the following individuals and organisations:

Project manager
Alison Proietto

Editor
Michelle Bennett

Author
Janine Scott

Cartographic advisor
Emily Maffei

Design and layout
Julie Hally of Penny Black Design

Index
Max McMaster

Pre-press
Splitting Image

Explore Australia Publishing Pty Ltd
Ground Floor, Building 1, 658 Church Street,
Richmond, VIC 3121

Explore Australia Publishing Pty Ltd is a division of
Hardie Grant Publishing Pty Ltd

hardie grant publishing

Published by Explore Australia Publishing Pty Ltd, 2015

Concept, text, maps, form and design © Explore Australia
Publishing Pty Ltd, 2015

A Cataloguing-in-Publication entry is available from the
catalogue of the National Library of Australia at www.nla.gov.au

The maps in this publication incorporate data © Commonwealth
of Australia (Geoscience Australia), 2015. Geoscience Australia
has not evaluated the data as altered and incorporated within
this publication, and therefore gives no warranty regarding
accuracy, completeness, currency or suitability for any
particular purpose.

ISBN-13 9781741174908

10 9 8 7 6 5 4 3 2 1

Printed and bound in China by 1010 Printing International Ltd

www.exploreaustralia.net.au
Follow us on Twitter: @ExploreAus
Find us on Facebook: www.facebook.com/exploreaustralia